Short-term contracts in social work

Library of Social Work

General Editor:
Noel Timms
Professor of Social Work Studies
University of Newcastle upon Tyne

Short-term contracts in social work

Joan M. Hutten
*Principal Social Worker and
Chairman of the Brief Focal Intervention Programme
Tavistock Clinic, London*

with:

Stella M. Hall
Elsie Osborne
Mannie Sher
Eva Sternberg
Elizabeth Tuters

Routledge & Kegan Paul
London, Henley and Boston

First published in 1977
by Routledge & Kegan Paul Ltd
39 Store Street,
London WC1E 7DD,
Broadway House,
Newtown Road,
Henley-on-Thames,
Oxon RG9 1EN and
9 Park Street,
Boston, Mass. 02108, USA
Set in 10 on 11pt English
and printed in Great Britain by
The Lavenham Press Limited
Lavenham, Suffolk

British Library Cataloguing in Publication Data

Hutten, Joan M

Short-term contracts in social work. —(Library
of social work).

1. Social service—Great Britain—Addresses,
essays, lectures
I. Title II. Series
361'. 941   HV245

ISBN 0-7100-8584-2
ISBN 0-7100-8585-0 Pbk
ISSN 0305-4381

Contents

Acknowledgments

Part I, chapter one appeared in *Social Work Today*, vol. IV, no. 22, 1974, pp. 709-11. Chapter two appeared in *Social Work Today*, vol. VI, no. 17, 1975, pp. 538-41. Chapter three and chapter four both appeared in *Social Work Today*, vol. 6, no. 20, 1976, pp. 614-19. Part 2, chapter six appeared in *Social Work Today*, vol. V, no. 8, 1974, pp. 226-31. All of these articles are reproduced, in some cases in an expanded version, by permission of the Editor, *Social Work Today*.

Part II, chapter three was originally published in *Social Work Service*, no. 7, July 1975, pp. 5-9, and is reproduced with the permission of the Controller of Her Majesty's Stationery Office.

I am indebted more than I know to all the colleagues whose work and thought has contributed to my formulations. I would like to record my gratitude to them and particularly to Elizabeth Tuters and Mary Barker who also wrote some of the case studies in my chapters.

Eva Sternberg wishes to acknowledge help received from Jean Leared, Professor F. Brill, Mrs Nurit Israeli and Mrs Therry Katz. Mannie Sher records his gratitude to Mrs Jane Temperley for the use of some of her case material. Stella Hall acknowledges the extensive contribution to the ongoing work with the Gibbs family of Janet Graham, Jean Schooling, Keith Small and Jane Symonds.

Finally I am indebted to Janice Uphill for her help with typing and collating the manuscript.

JMH

The contributors

Stella M. Hall was at the time this work was undertaken principal social worker, Adolescent Department, Tavistock Clinic, London.

Joan M. Hutten is principal social worker and chairman of the Brief Focal Intervention Programme in the Department for Children and Parents, Tavistock Clinic, London.

Elsie Osborne is principal educational psychologist, Department for Children and Parents, Tavistock Clinic, London.

Mannie Sher was at the time the work described was undertaken a senior social worker member of the adult psychotherapy training course in the Adult Department, Tavistock Clinic, London.

Eva Sternberg is senior social worker, Mental Health Clinic, Ramatchen, Tel Aviv University Medical School. She spent a sabbatical year attached to the Brief Focal Intervention Programme in the Department for Children and Parents, Tavistock Clinic, and returned to Israel shortly before the outbreak of war.

Elizabeth Tuters was at the time the work described was undertaken a senior social worker working in the Brief Focal Intervention Programme in the Department for Children and Parents, Tavistock Clinic, London.

Introduction

In 1971 I was invited by my colleagues in the department for children and parents at the Tavistock Clinic to initiate a programme of brief focal intervention with service, teaching and research responsibilities. Its human resources would consist in a proportion of the professional time of a small number of psychiatrists, psychologists, child psychotherapists and social workers, all committed to sharing and reviewing their experience in this field by attending an ongoing workshop and, we hoped, by writing.

Psychological testing has only been carried out by educational psychologists but assessment and treatment of either the whole family or the individual members has been carried out by any and all of the disciplines as available. Allocation of cases to the programme after preliminary exploration by a member of an intake group has become more confident as we have clarified for ourselves and others the kind of referrals that can usefully be dealt with in this way. It goes without saying that many cases might also have been helped had they been allocated to a programme specializing in intensive, individual or in family therapy, but, in the interests of offering a model to be tried for size by practitioners in other agencies, we now offer you the results of looking for brief focal opportunities and applying techniques that have seemed valid in terms of our understanding so far.

The Tavistock is a metropolitan teaching clinic. It has resources and sanction to use time in a way that many social workers might find enviable. What can possibly come out of such an institution that can speak to the condition of social workers in hard-pressed agencies in this country and abroad?

I can only say that I am very aware of this dilemma, but have also had very warming experiences of discovering that common problems and a common language do emerge when a dialogue is started. In particular I am grateful for the confirmation I have received progressively from the social workers from a wide range of agencies who have attended my one year part-time seminar courses during the last five years. These qualified and experienced workers come to the Tavistock to share their experiences and to carve out for themselves a little space each week, away from their work situation, in which they can reflect on and try to learn from the work challenges to which they are exposed. They are motivated to sharpen their assessment skills and to explore ways of becoming more effective in the casework aspects of their jobs. They have constituted my touchstone of actuality in social work. I have written for them and refined with them. The fact that the multifarious problems that they brought could be illuminated by the formulations that I and my colleagues were developing out of our experience in a clinical setting has been an important validation. This process was taken a stage further when, during the spring of 1976, I was invited to discuss my own contributions to this book with the multidisciplinary staff group of a local authority mental health clinic in Perugia, Italy. In an exchange of views lasting over twelve hours of seminar discussions, the relevance and applicability of short-term contract concepts was very convincingly experienced.

The rapid social and technological changes of the 1960s, followed by the economic vicissitudes of the 1970s have created a context in which, although the need for a long-term perspective has become more important, the need for a flexible system of response to changing intercurrent challenges has made both the social and mental health services and their clients eager to search for appropriate short-term interventions. The present volume is offered as a basis for discussion. Further digestion and clarification will inevitably take place but, for the moment, we need to know what use a wider range of consumers can make of the thinking and practice we present.

Part I of the book includes the working papers that were part blueprint for and part a review of the development of a specialized programme for brief focal intervention in the department for children and parents at the Tavistock Clinic. The thinking and the practice refreshed each other in turn.

Part II of the book contains contributions first from colleagues who have collaborated in the work of the programme, each one making their own applications and interweaving the commonly developed formulations with their own pre-existing body of theory, and second from colleagues who have independently arrived at very comparable formulations out of work done in other departments of the clinic.

Part one

Developing a theory

Joan M. Hutten

Chapter one

A rationale for brief focal intervention by social workers

Listening to social workers, one cannot for long avoid a mental image of beleaguered troops surrounded by clamouring hordes of clients. Will the food and water supplies last until a new harvest brings temporarily renewed hope? Or will worker and client alike die of famine in an unviably organized society?

Social work interventions that are brief and focal (and effective) seem as illusory as the philosopher's stone. Are there any magical short cuts or is there real theoretical backing for the discipline of planned short-term work?

Before I review the references that seem to me to support the validity of this strategy, I suggest that one principle of social work intervention ought to be that of helping the client to *reflect* on his situation and the available options so that he can *choose* which one is most satisfying and acceptable (to self, status group and society). This process is both ego-enhancing and affirming of growth potential. The compulsive care-giving that characterizes much of social work tends to reduce the client's autonomy and engenders dependency and hostility. If one is to harness a valuable impulse to care to the needs of those with appropriate dependency needs and to distinguish those for whom the nurturing of growth potential by 'standing by' rather than by 'doing for' is appropriate (Miller (Miller and Gwynne, 1972) in his book about residential homes for the handicapped describes the pitfalls of both poles of this dimension very vividly), a basic diagnostic skill is essential together with some conviction about the value of work-review.

Diagnosis and review

In making a diagnosis one reviews the family constellation with names and ages, and the facts of historical and current explanatory

3

importance; establishes what is the present crisis, what stresses are operating, what strengths and resources are available. One monitors the response to interpretation or to the experience of relationship in the interview as an indication of what kind of help the client is able to use. At any given point the information available is incomplete but willy nilly plans and predictions are made on inadequate information and the excuse that more knowledge is needed before the worker's judgment of the situation can be crystallized and recorded is a lazy subterfuge whose only effect is to make the worker feel more burdened and busy and the client more confused and inadequate. A crisp summary of the worker's understanding of referral information and the rationale of the proposed first step is something that is done, thoughtfully or by default, more often than it is recorded. A similar crisp summary of the exploratory phase of contact with a tentative plan for intervention and the goals set is another useful landmark that serves as the punctuation for the contact. The preservation of breathing/thinking space around the worker and the client is a requisite for survival. At this point it may be necessary to establish a contract for an assessment period of defined length or it may already be possible to establish an agreement to work together on a specific problem or constellation of problems with periodic review planned and with either ending or change of contract required.

A review of the literature

If this degree of discipline feels a military imposition, perhaps it may help it to appear congenial and voluntarily adoptable if we review some of the work that underpins it.

Erikson's (1965) psycho-social definition of the eight stages of development, which relate to Freud's psycho-biological formulation, gives a hierarchical model for diagnosis and for assessment of growth. No growth is achieved once and for all, stress induces regression and affirmed coping facilitates natural growth. If one assesses a family or an individual on the dimensions of basic trust versus mistrust; autonomy versus shame and doubt; initiative versus guilt; industry versus inferiority; identity versus role-confusion; intimacy versus isolation; generativity versus stagnation; ego-integrity versus despair, it is then possible to determine at intervals whether the input of service has had effect in the desired direction or whether a re-evaluation of the strategy of intervention is required. Many social resources are applied wantonly and wastefully with no monitoring of results and it would seem infinitely preferable that the worker accept responsibility for monitoring the effectiveness or appropriateness of his strategy rather than that the holder of

4

resources, whether financial, personal, medical or housing, resorts to a punitive condemning of the *client* for a misuse of resources.

Reid and Shyne's (1969) research comparing the effectiveness of planned short-term intervention with open-ended treatment for randomly selected clients at a family agency surprised the researchers by the conclusiveness of the evidence in favour of the former.

Geismar (1969), discussing the strategies for preventive intervention in social work, divides prevention into primary, secondary and tertiary levels. Primary prevention corresponds in the social sphere to the concept of public health in medicine; appropriate measures for achieving this would be adequate dissemination of information about rights and resources, social action to ensure community health and adequate rights and resources. We speak of secondary prevention when we describe appropriate measures for surmounting incipient problems and the whole of crisis theory is relevant to this level of intervention. Tertiary prevention relates to attempts to stabilize, avoid deterioration or effect rehabilitation in situations of well established social pathology.

Leonard (1971) has discussed the challenge of primary prevention helpfully in relation to the value system of social work. Our emphasis on the individual as end as well as means in society, implies that it is important to share with the client our diagnosis not only of internal personality and family dynamics but also of external contributions to his problem. This need to *communicate* our assessment, to ourselves, to our clients, to our colleagues and to politicians and society at large is an inalienable responsibility for those who are committed to helping and to prevention.

The concept of crisis

To return to secondary prevention and crisis theory, Caplan (1961) has adumbrated the concept of crisis, pleasant or unpleasant, the result of normal personal growth or of untoward circumstance, as a moment when new patterns of behaviour have to be devised which may lead, optimally, to greater confidence and flexibility when future crises are encountered or to greater rigidity, limitation and maladaptation as successive crises are unsuccessfully confronted. Social work can very profitably exploit the potential for growth and learning that is inherent in any early problem situation. A child manifesting symptoms of distress at starting school may evoke social work intervention which gives both him and his mother and the school some insight into separation anxieties so that a successful resolution may serve as a reference point of successful growth and adaptation when future anxieties are encountered. Failure to surmount that crisis may lead only to personality restriction,

5

timidity and poor performance if no effective intervention is available and further experiences are reassuring. If no intervention is available and further experiences reinforce anxiety, the child may go through school-refusal to work-refusal and illiteracy with society intervening in increasingly heroic, expensive and unsuccessful ways.

Has brief focal intervention any rationale for confronting situations where tertiary prevention is all that can be hoped for?

The reference which I have found meaningful in this connection is the beautifully recorded, almost literary, self-portraits that emerge in Lewis's (1962 and 1968) studies of the culture of poverty in Mexico and in Puerto Rico. He approached his subjects as an anthropologist simply wanting to know what life for the individual members of one family was like. What emerges is a monument to the capacity of the most under-privileged to reflect on and relate to the continuity of their own experience. If we as social workers can resist the compulsion to take the problems of others on our own shoulders, we may learn a great deal about the capacity of the human spirit to transcend handicap and to use an empathic listener as an auxiliary ego in a predominantly id-organized life pattern. If our multi-problem clients are to achieve dignity and increased mastery it is our affirmation of their right to choose this rather than our determination to thrust it on them that is relevant. In brief intervention terms it is their right to use appropriate help or to reject temporarily un-acceptable solutions that enhances their coping repertoire. Our time perspective and the clients' must often be at variance. How often, I wonder, is a decision to do 'long-term supportive work' a joint decision with the client rather than a collusive compliance with minimal consensus between worker and client goals?

The issue of social control

This introduces the issue of social control—an issue passionately debated by social workers in post-Seebohm social services departments. Are social workers instruments of society for the control or elimination of inconvenient behaviour? Are they rather advocates for the inarticulate and misunderstood? It is the need to find an acceptable stance that holds the rights of individuals and of society in a functional relationship that make my next reference particularly relevant.

McGregor (1960) developed a theory of human relations in industry which subsequent students have found relevant and extendable. Its relevance to social work emerges with compelling freshness for not being couched in helping profession jargon. If one thinks of an input-process-output model of social work, the desirability of achieving congruent personal, social and economic goals is not unlike the task of maximizing work satisfaction and productivity in industry. McGregor contrasts theory X and theory Y assumptions: according to theory X average man dislikes work and will avoid it—therefore there is a need for coercion and threat of punishment. Average man prefers to be directed, avoids responsibility, has little ambition and values security above all.

Theory Y, on the other hand, postulates that work is natural; self-direction and self-control are possible; commitment to objectives is related to ego satisfactions; average man under proper conditions seeks responsibility; the capacity to use imagination and creativity is widespread and intellectual potential is only partially realized.

It seems likely that some at least of social workers' anxieties about social control arise because of confusion about the coherence of theory Y so that a strategy which unwittingly subscribes in part to one theory and in part to the other feels acutely uncomfortable and is doomed to failure. At least if the worker is alert to the conflict in the two approaches he can devise a coherent plan of intervention—if he can secure an appropriate context for theory Y he can achieve within that context. If theory X values so permeate the client's situation that the social worker cannot achieve enough 'space' for theory Y tactics it is advantageous to recognize this and to address efforts to changing the context rather than to waste efforts on frustrating self and client in any inherently impossible undertaking. The theory is also rich in applications for the social work agency, and the influence of social workers' job satisfaction and enthusiasm on the outcome of their work with clients is another topic of relevance to brief focal work.

Malan (1963) in his research into brief psychotherapy came to the conclusion that maintenance of therapeutic enthusiasm was a crucial factor in successful work. Goldberg (1970) in her research into the relative success of untrained and professionally trained workers in helping the aged demonstrated a significantly higher rate of success in the first half of the study when the workers were enthused with the new project. Perhaps this is one element in the Reid and Shyne finding that planned short-term work was more successful than open-ended treatment. Worker boredom and apathy may often pass unrecognized—it is easy to blame the client for outwitting ill-conceived interventions.

If I seem to castigate current social work practice, my aim is only to address myself to social work as it is, not as it might be. To idealize the profession is to do it no service. Greater skill does come with age and experience to those who continue to keep in touch with reality and it is the task of the profession to devise both organizations and staff development programmes that do relate to real and changing needs effectively. Brief focal intervention seems to relate to reality in so far as intermediate goals congruent with long-term aspirations are all it is possible to plan for realistically. If short-term goals are not achieved it is realistic to review the diagnostic and prognostic formulation and to make more appropriate recommendations for the next phase.

The importance of shared goals

Far from saying that all problems are soluble in a short time if workers are only skilled enough, I am saying that professional time is best invested towards the achievement of shared goals and it is more blessed to stop and admit the need for a correction in plan than to assume a mutual goal that doesn't exist. Meyer and Timms (1970) in their research into consumer satisfaction with social work found greatest dissatisfaction where there was greatest distance between client and worker goals; crudely, where the client felt he needed material help and information and the worker felt the client needed insight into problems he was unaware of.

So far we have made an argument for brief contracts and intermediate goals. What about the focus? Just as the two year probation order may lend itself to a brief piece of work in relation to a lifetime of problem-solving, so the single interview may be significant for the migrant in crisis who will be a thousand miles away tomorrow. Focus, as photographers will know, is related to different depths of vision. Focus may be sternly concrete or multi-relevantly abstract but it must be shared. The client's challenge to the social worker is how much of my real problem and its context can you understand and how much of your understanding can you share with me?

Chapter two

Indications and opportunities for brief focal intervention

When time is limited by outside factors

Clients who refer themselves just before they are due to emigrate, leave home or go on holiday seem to find the courage to seek help only when the deadline really feels imminent and some decision can no longer be postponed or avoided by being busy.

Mr and Mrs Grey had decided to separate; what they couldn't decide was who should have their 18-month-old daughter. Mr Grey would be returning to his family in South Africa and Mrs Grey would be staying in London. They had 'failed' as a couple; was there any way in which they could 'succeed' as parents by coming to a joint decision in the best interests of their child? From the start, the psychotherapist who saw them made it clear that she would not advise them, she would only try to help them explore and understand the problem so that they might be better able to make their own decision. A year previously, Mrs Grey had formed a relationship with the man with whom she was now proposing to live. Mr Grey had been hurt and upset and didn't want her to leave. Her guilt made her feel that it would only be fair to leave their child with him. Both were very fond of her and had shared the parenting so that both agreed that she would be well taken care of by either. In the few meetings that there was time for they explored the pain in the situation for both of them and rang up to cancel the last appointment. A few days later Mr Grey wrote that they had together reached the decision that their daughter should remain with her mother, that he still had to struggle with his feelings about the loss but was grateful for help which had enabled them to share the decision in the interests of the child rather than at the expense of the child.

The reluctant client

The reluctant client, who makes both referees and agency staff here

9

and elsewhere feel ultra-responsible, presents in a variety of ways but wants help only on his own (impossible) terms. Here the focal task is to explore what, if any, contract can be made. The worker can often only guess what may be the reasons for, on the face of it, a totally irrational mistrust. Does reluctance stem from an earlier, bad experience of a similar agency, from family-determined expectations of society at large or of people of the worker's age/sex/profession in particular? What skeletons mustn't come out of the cupboard? Is the need to dominate, frustrate, manipulate the environment a reaction to stress or a persistent character trait which there is no incentive to change?

We have had a number of cases who were in no way ready to share responsibility for the outcome of the contact with the clinic at the outset, whose experience of brief focal intervention enabled them to make a responsible commitment to work on their difficulties over time. Kai and his family were one of these.

Mr and Mrs Kenyon are in their early thirties and although separated for over a year, together contacted the clinic regarding their 7-year-old son and only child, who was living with Mrs Kenyon. Both parents felt concern for Kai's adjustment and progress at school and at home. He seemed shy, sad and unhappy, had few friends and was unable to do maths. The Kenyons wanted something for their son and, they thought, for themselves, but were unsure what and whether they could in fact trust anyone as they both had had so many bad experiences from their childhood and with the mental health professions to date. They wanted to be told what to do yet reserve the right to say it was unsuitable.

Both parents were themselves only children from broken homes. Mr Kenyon's family is middle-class professional and his parents were together until he was six, then Mr Kenyon lived with his mother, who maintained a gypsy existence until, as a teenager, he lived with his remarried father up to his own marriage to Mrs Kenyon. As an adolescent, Mr Kenyon was very troubled and for four years was involved in individual therapy followed by two years of group therapy which he attended with his future wife. They became involved and she became pregnant with Kai. At first they planned a termination but waited too long and finally married, deciding that was what they had both wanted. The early years together were happy and ideal.

Mrs Kenyon is Swedish and was adopted at three months. She believes her natural mother to be a professional nurse but has no information about her natural father. Her adoptive parents were working class, unable to have children of their own, for reasons unknown. Mrs Kenyon's recall of her childhood is of closeness to both parents separately yet always sleeping in her parents' bedroom to protect her mother from violent attacks from her father when he was drunk. When she was 14 her father left the home, never to be seen or heard from again. Mrs Kenyon subsequently became involved in a series of pregnancies with no awareness why. Her first was terminated by a ghastly home procedure, as she was refused a legal abortion, being over age. For her second and third pregnancies she was again denied state termination and so had both babies in a state institution for unwed mothers giving both up for adoption, sight unseen. Having disgraced her mother throughout all of this, she left Sweden with a boy friend and came to England where she met her husband at a rowdy, brawling party. It was love at first sight according to both.

When first seen at the clinic, the Kenyons were feeling a great deal of pain for their son's position and their own past histories, but were sceptical, mistrusting, angry and defensive. They felt communication a problem with Kai, with each other and with the clinic. They wanted something but they knew not what. They felt all three to be merged into one big sticky mess. Since the marriage break-up, Mr Kenyon had gone into psychoanalysis, yet felt he needed something separate for his son and his wife as they all felt themselves to be so fused and tangled.

Because of their complicated backgrounds and the confusion with which they presented themselves, the strategy considered appropriate and indeed shared with the Kenyons was to begin a series of meetings with a social worker who would become engaged with them at their level of apprehension and confusion. The three adults would become involved in an attempt to tease out (a) what in fact *were* the problems, and (b) what were the possible ways of dealing with the problems identified. The contract was set for weekly meetings of an undetermined number until such time the problems had been located and the methods of dealing with them mutually decided upon. This extensive exploratory phase took fifteen weeks during which time Kai was identified as having problems that required assessment. Psychological tests were jointly decided upon and administered and the results were shared with the child and parents together by the psychologist during the parents' meeting with the social worker.

The focus of the work then was with the parents to enable them to make a responsible decision about the next step, where they went from here. The psychological tests indicated intensive psychotherapy as the treatment of choice for Kai's problems. This recommendation became another problem for the parents to focus on and work at, as their own past experiences with treatment had been so unsatisfactory. After another nine sessions exploring alternatives, among which was family therapy, the parents decided they wanted their son to have intensive individual treatment, and were prepared to wait until such

11

a resource became available. They themselves chose to continue as a couple with the social worker to work on their own problems, particularly as experienced in their marriage, in order to discover what went wrong, could it be put right or was it really over. They wanted to explore their relationship at least to understand it so as not to repeat it again.

At present the child has attended four times weekly for intensive therapy over the past six months. The parents are being seen together weekly. Both the parents' and the child's therapist see the therapy lasting for several years with marked benefit. The father has continued in his own analysis with observable gains; the mother has recently made a decision to begin once a week individual therapy for herself and to pay privately. Both wish to continue on at the clinic as a couple for as long as Kai is in treatment. They feel they have made unmeasurable gains for themselves as parents, as a marital couple and as people. They continue to live apart but in a much more controlled, self-sufficient way and anticipate the likelihood of divorce. Both feel they and their child now have a chance and a choice in life and living and are not completely caught by their past history and family circumstances.

Others, like Jeremy and his family, have discovered that a limited contract was possible and worthwhile.

Jeremy Anderson, aged 11 years, 4 months, was the eldest son of Mr Anderson aged 55 and Mrs Anderson aged 38. He had two brothers aged 10 and 9. At the beginning of the Spring term, Jeremy was referred to the clinic by his school headteacher, who thought him to be 'on the verge of a nervous breakdown'. The referral was supported by the family doctor.

The initial assessment interview with the mother and father revealed a behaviour change in Jeremy four months prior, following a bout of 'flu and his maternal grandmother's unexpected death. Jeremy had suddenly become weepy and withdrawn, the school said solitary and antisocial. Both parents were irritated and distressed by the school's referral and did not agree with the school's assessment of Jeremy's mental state. Although the Andersons felt angry and defensive they showed concern for their son's reported difficulties. They thought he might be reacting to a series of events and agreed to continue meeting together, with Jeremy, to explore his problems with a team composed of a social worker and psychologist.

The first appointment offered was attended late and only by Mr Anderson and Jeremy. Mrs Anderson had attended a meeting concerned with rehousing. The family was inadequately housed in two rooms, all family members shared the same bedroom. The father considered *this* to be the basis of Jeremy's difficulties and nothing to do with the school, the area we had suggested we might explore. Mr Anderson announced he had no time for such nonsense, asked his son to come along and left saying his wife would contact us as Jeremy thought he might like to return to the clinic. She did do, and we subsequently offered a series of five weekly appointments all of which were cancelled indirectly at the last minute, yet always a request was received for another one. To determine our strategy and how we might be of help to the Andersons we contacted the relevant network, the school, doctor and social services department.

The school reported Jeremy was so troublesome, fighting, leaving class and truanting, that he was in danger of suspension. The doctor spoke highly of the Anderson boys and Mr Anderson, and admitted that although he had attended all boys since birth and treated Mr Anderson for angina, he had never seen Mrs Anderson. He believed the Andersons to have a stable co-habitee relationship and to be the natural parents of the boys—yet he knew the Anderson name to be an alias, that Mr Anderson had a hidden past and had been charged with exhibitionism. The social services department was currently involved in the rehousing issue with the Andersons with the doctor's support, yet found them to be standoffish and defensive, wanting no help whatsoever.

One month after the first dramatic meeting with Jeremy and his father, Jeremy and his mother arrived for their appointment late. The school had in the meantime suspended Jeremy, yet both mother and son insisted it was by mutual agreement and because of a misunderstanding.

Jeremy, throughout the session, appeared depressed and spoke of his feelings of hopelessness and despair. He stuttered badly and bit his finger nails. He longed for more space and a new school yet felt it was all in vain. He agreed to come back *only* if his brothers did not know and did not come.

Both mother and son thought an appropriate focus would be on Jeremy's school difficulties and agreed to a contract for eight weekly meetings to include the father over the next two months and to have Jeremy take psychological tests for the purpose of deciding on the best school placement for him as he was in his final year of primary school. The mother felt the housing was none of our concern and refused any offer of help. Mrs Anderson and Jeremy kept all arranged appointments. They arrived twenty minutes late, never together and never with Mr Anderson. Apologies and excuses were always given for absence and lateness, and the subject dropped. As Jeremy and the psychologist worked on test material, Mrs Anderson and the social worker met together. Mrs Anderson remained defensive and lighthearted, seeing improvement and underestimating any problems of hers, the family's or Jeremy's.

For the reporting back of the psychological tests session, the father joined Jeremy and his mother. Jeremy was found to be of high average intelligence but underachieving and with emotional difficulties. His behaviour during testing was reluctant, resistant, hesitant and obsessive. The recommendation made was for placement in a school for maladjusted children, which the parents and Jeremy reacted violently against and flatly refused to accept. They requested a further series of meetings to explore and work out a more suitable school alternative. We re-negotiated a second contract for six more weekly meetings until summer break with both parents to attend with Jeremy, which they did do.

The father very much took the role of leader and focuser throughout this second series, with mother and Jeremy understating any problems. The school placement was dealt with immediately by Jeremy being accepted by a comprehensive school of the Andersons' choice. The next area focused on by the father was Jeremy's stutter. They explored the possibility of arranging speech therapy through the school, but father and mother decided it was not the speech that was causing Jeremy's emotional problems, as Jeremy would like it to be, but the other way round.

Mr Anderson then brought up the problem of the father-son relationship and Jeremy's lack of confidence in himself and his preference to always be with his father. Both parents felt they expected Jeremy to act much older than his years and maybe were robbing him of his youth, thereby contributing to the fights amongst the brothers.

A family pattern was identified of the parents talking for Jeremy and never listening to what he had to say. Jeremy's stutter had become less evident throughout the sessions, and in the penultimate session he shared his secret worries to do with the supernatural and how he always felt his parents wanted to be rid of him until they took the firm stand they did over refusing to allow him to be sent to a school for maladjusted children.

By the end of the second contract, the Andersons reviewed the improvement in Jeremy and in their family functioning in general. They had all decided to listen to each other. The school was finding Jeremy settled and happy again and the Andersons had received confirmation of being rehoused. The two younger brothers were still considered a problem as far as the school was concerned, however not as far as the parents were concerned.

The Andersons found termination difficult, evidence that they found the clinic experience to be a positive one in the end. They knew they were welcome to return at any time for whatever reason and that re-contacting the clinic was considered to be their responsibility. Their subsequent brief contact with the clinic will be alluded to later.

Yet others, like the Towns and Frederick, have been helped to withdraw from a non-useful association with the agency without feeling rejecting or rejected.

Mrs Town, a 40-year-old mother of two boys, Frederick 9 and Jonathan 13, contacted the clinic regarding her younger son's learning problem, his inability to read and his bedwetting. Mrs Town and her cohabitee of seven years, Dr Urquhart, had had contact with a clinic psychiatrist several years ago regarding the elder boy's manifest behaviour problem. This contact ended abruptly and without satisfaction for the boy, Mrs Town, Dr Urquhart or the clinic as the help which the family had wanted and the help the clinic offered at that time seemed divergent.

Considering this unfortunate past history, the strategy considered appropriate this time was to offer them an assessment phase and to form an initial team of social worker and educational psychologist, in the light of the expressed educational problems. These together offered to see the entire family in order to sort out past from present and identify the unit of attention at the moment.

The first appointment offered the family was failed with no reply until after the appointment date when Mrs Town rang up leaving a message for the educational psychologist only, to say that they could not make the time offered. The team responded to this communication as locating the focus for their unit of attention. The mother appeared interested only in educational advice, and so the amended strategy was to have the educational psychologist contact Mrs Town and offer to see Frederick for psychological testing for the purpose of shedding light on his reading difficulties.

The mother responded enthusiastically, agreed in principle to the testing, accepted the three appointments offered, then subsequently cancelled two requesting alternative times. Finally, upon completion of these tests Mrs Town, Dr Urquhart and Frederick were offered a series of three appointments by the initial team in order that they might discuss the test results in full. Mrs Town arrived for the first of the scheduled meetings without Frederick and Dr Urquhart joined her towards the end. She was in a harried state and talked non-stop. She felt herself responsible for all of her boys' problems, particularly for Frederick's bedwetting as she babied him. She did wonder, however, if his reading difficulties had to do entirely with her or also with his natural father, who had a reading problem, even though the boys seldom saw their father as she separated from him eight years ago. When Dr Urquhart arrived, he looked worried and dishevelled and confused. He had been detained at the university where he taught chemistry. Both questioned the wisdom of having Frederick present and thought it best to leave him at home.

For the second meeting, both Mrs Town and Dr Urquhart were on time and seemed more relaxed, at ease and composed. They listened attentively to the psychologist's findings. Frederick was a boy of above average intelligence who had a definite problem with reading that troubled him but rather than deal with it directly he tried desperately hard to conceal it from himself and others by most complicated manoeuvres, which took most of his time to construct and much of his mental energy to execute. Both Mrs Town and Dr Urquhart recognized Frederick's functioning immediately as being familiar and discussed ways they might help him. Mrs Town had already arranged for reading tutorials for Frederick which he loathed, yet she found with firm handling on her part he attended and actually was beginning to read. Dr Urquhart wondered if extra reading classes were enough and enquired whether something more was required.

For the third and last of the scheduled meetings, Frederick accompanied his mother and Dr Urquhart. He was carrying school books with him. He chose to sit on the floor throughout the session, at first as a defiant angry gesture, but became more positively involved as the session progressed. He said he did not like *not* reading and wished he could. When Dr Urquhart asked him directly how we could help him, Frederick turned to Dr Urquhart and told him he wished when he came to him with a word he could not read that Dr Urquhart would stop saying 'sound it'—that Frederick said, made him cross and angry and he wanted never to ask or try again. Both Mrs Town and Dr Urquhart listened carefully to Frederick's complaints and resolved to try to handle things differently in the future.

They thanked us for the help they had received, felt satisfied and able to handle the rest themselves. Informal follow-up information a year later showed that Frederick had improved very considerably in all areas of school functioning and bedwetting was reduced.

It is always helpful to remember that life itself poses a series of problems for all of us and often it is only when we professionals can reduce our irrational wish to do such a good and complete piece of work that the client will never again need help that we can begin to see what limited but worthwhile intervention *is* possible. Some clients are only able to get into a position of being able to use help by the experience of not having it rammed down their throats.

Sudden loss by death or separation

When people die of old age or after a prolonged illness, there is mourning work to be done inevitably but there has been time for anticipatory work, a coming to terms with part of what the loss will mean, a reviewing of common memories, sometimes together, and at least some start on the process of integrating both good and bad experiences so that life can go on unrestricted by scar-formation. When death or loss by separation comes suddenly in the midst of life, the crisis for the survivors has to be met without preparation. Within the family, for each member the loss will have a different significance and each one's capacity to enter imaginatively into the distress of the others may be reduced by his own pain. The need to initiate immediate changes, to cope adequately with the material situation means that recognition of the time needed for the process of mourning gets postponed and finally feels incongruous and inappropriate. The Visha case-study later in this book is one illustration of this.

The Norris family also had this experience. The father's work took him for some months to a tropical island. His wife and children joined him for the summer holidays but their happiness together was abruptly shattered by the mother's sudden death following a snake-bite in spite of being flown to another island for hospital treatment. The father accompanied his wife and had several days of increasing hopelessness without being able to communicate either with his unconscious wife or with his children who were left in the care of friends. After the death he 'phoned the friends, saying he would like to break the news to the children himself. The children were told that their father was returning alone but the younger girl managed to believe that both parents would be returning together. The need to complete the work contract, to cope suddenly with the entire responsibility for the children, to arrange for the return to England and the re-organization of work and living arrangements so that he could sustain the remaining family group together was only possible in a state of numbed misery. At first the children repeated their catastrophic experience to school friends, relatives and neighbours without any resolution of their pain. The ordinariness of everyday living took over and it was only when one child developed chest pains without physical cause and the other became moody and slept badly six months later, that the father sought help for himself and his family. The pain and desperation he was feeling as he recounted the past experience and his present dilemmas conveyed itself poignantly. A family interview was arranged with an agency team that had not previously worked together. To the family's surprise, it was the most stoical child who broke down and wept for them all and it was the sensitive response of the father which enabled them to collect themselves together to face school and work again before leaving. Their expectation that the 'experts' would 'put them at ease' and 'know the answers' was not fulfilled, instead they experienced us as 'awkward' and 'at a loss'. Following this meeting both children were given projective tests by the psychologist on the team and the father met twice with the social worker. His own feeling that he was a poor talker was repeatedly disproved as he reviewed his own and the children's situation articulately and allowed his mind to play round the possible future alternatives. At a final family meeting with the whole team to discuss the test findings, each member responded with his or her own observations and experiences and it seemed as though this opportunity to be listened to by us and by each other enabled the essential continuity of their life before the loss, since and for the future, with all the mixed feelings of love and anger involved, to be found again. They felt ready to work out hopeful plans for the future, no longer totally constrained by an unresolved past.

Potentially chronic clients

How much psychosis is around in this family? What are realistic goals for a multiply disadvantaged and handicapped family? As social workers (and others!) have found to their cost, it is not difficult to attract a burdensome, unrewarding case-load of chronic clients, whose chronicity is as much determined by the professionals' behaviour as by the 'defects' of the client. Angry dependency of client on worker or of worker on clients is not a worthwhile way of passing time or being busy.

Mrs Millen approached the clinic because her neighbour, a professional woman who had received help for her own marital problems, considered that one of Mrs Millen's grandchildren was more aggressive than he should be and this aroused her own ever-present anxieties. With some difficulty she described her complicated family situation which involved three generations of divorce, illegitimacy and mental illness, up to now contained by modest affluence, education, good works and 'respectability'. This was not a situation that could be made 'normal' and 'healthy' by any professional magic wand. It was decided to offer four appointments for all members of the household to review their situation with a psychiatrist and a social worker. Permission was refused for a school visit to obtain independent observations of the cousin-grandchildren's relationships with other children and with adults. The family's behaviour in the interview situation was commented on in relation to the incidents described at home. The real difficulties for grand-mother and daughter/mother/aunt, both deserted by their menfolk in bringing up their male grandchildren/son/nephew, were clarified and discussed. Fears of breakdown, of domination, of bad inheritance, of psychiatry were openly talked about and the not inconsiderable achievements of this interdependent group were acknowledged and valued. I think it would be true to say that they concluded their meetings feeling more secure in their coping and that any of them could approach the clinic at any time of stress in the future without fearing that professionals might want to take over their lives or proffer unacceptable advice. It is now two years since this intervention and there is reason to believe that the doctor would have alerted us to any crisis, had the family themselves not been able to do so.

The case of Peter is another example of appropriate relating to the adult, coping capacity in a family dealing with an inescapable handicap that may not be as globally hopeless as mere labelling might imply.

In the spring term, Mrs Gunn, an Irish working-class mother, approached the school doctor at the school for the educationally sub-normal, to which her 11½-year-old son, Peter, had been transferred six months earlier. She was concerned over his lack of progress, his behaviour problem and inability to learn. This school doctor had known Mrs Gunn through welfare clinics since the birth of her eldest son, Jason, now 16, and her daughter, Paulette, now 14 and the doctor had arranged tests for Peter at the children's hospital following his birth and subsequently as he had seemed slow to progress. The test results confirmed he was brain-damaged and a school for the educationally subnormal was recommended and he was placed on a waiting list.

Peter and Mrs Gunn were unhappy with the school, it was a long distance from the home and Peter had trouble getting to it. In the school Peter was a problem, refusing to do work and fighting with others. The school initiated the referral to the clinic as they were at a loss as to what to do for Peter and his mother.

In the clinic, Mrs Gunn was at first seen by a social worker. Her main worry was that Peter was wrongly placed in the school system. She maintained she had never been fully told the test results and had no true picture of Peter's capabilities and potential. Her husband, a truck driver, had been off work for several months with undiagnosed eye complaints, but when we began an assessment process for Peter at the clinic he returned to work, thereby refusing to attend meetings.

Mrs Gunn and Peter were seen for an extensive assessment phase of thirteen sessions which involved receiving reports from all of the network contacts to date; having a child psychiatrist join for several meetings to give a medical opinion and arranging for a psychologist to retest Peter after he fully explained to them what he would be doing and why. When the tests were completed, the results were discussed with mother and Peter, father also attended but reluctantly —making it clear he was losing valuable time from work and considered Peter a 'cabbage' regardless of clinic opinion.

Peter was found to be brain damaged and considered well placed in his present school. He could learn to read and write but only with great difficulty and pain. Both Mrs Gunn and Peter responded to this opinion as a sign of hope and wanted more help but did not know of what nature.

Mrs Gunn met alone with the social worker for a series of four sessions to enable her to explore the problems she felt she faced and to decide on the area for further attention. She looked at her poor marital relationship and the poor father-son relationship but decided she could do nothing about either as she felt so indebted to her husband who faithfully stood by her after Peter's birth when she was so depressed and actually suicidal. Mrs Gunn did acknowledge there was considerable sibling rivalry between Peter and her other two children and considered this an area accessible to help, by directly involving the children, herself and her husband, but she knew they would not come to the clinic. The social worker and psychologist negotiated a series of five meetings in the home with what family members could be present; the focus to be on Peter and the family's understanding of his problems. All attended except father who occasionally joined at the end. Throughout the sessions Peter revealed how 'horrible' it felt inside to know there was something wrong with your brain—his mother, brother and sister had never heard Peter talk about how he felt and how 'awful' it was not to know how to read and write. They acknowledged they felt 'awful' themselves and dealt with Peter *as if* the pain he felt would go away some day because his pain stirred up such helpless pain in them that they could do nothing about it except defend against it by denial. All of the family then became involved in trying to find ways to help Peter rather than continue to deny their pain. At the same time, they let Peter know how difficult he could be and how frustrating to them by some of his moods, and he shared similar feelings with them.

By the fifth and last session everyone, including Peter, felt better and more confident to deal with their problems themselves. They felt they no longer needed clinic help. A six month follow-up meeting was suggested by the team and was responded to enthusiastically by Peter.

Since then there have been two such six month follow-up meetings. In the first, all the family was present—and a change in all was observable. Peter himself was happy, had slimmed down, been promoted in school, could tie his shoes and was beginning to read. Mother had lost two stone and had taken a part-time job. Father saw a change in Peter and no longer felt he was a 'cabbage'. The other two children were doing well in school and were pleased with Peter and their understanding of him. The family appeared much closer and better functioning.

In the second six month follow-up, the progress noted with Peter had continued. He could read and do sums and tell the time. He had a much better self-concept and proudly told of his morning paper round and the Saturday job he was seeking. He liked school and hoped to become an electrician. Mother was finding Paulette more of a problem now than Peter as she was moody and rebellious. Both Mr and Mrs Gunn had had chronic recurrent illness; Mr Gunn had been off work for six months with a slipped disc, Mrs Gunn had an eye haemorrhage but despite these health problems, the family was continuing to function and cope with their own problems in an appropriate way. Peter has again asked for a further six month follow-up.

Breakdown in communication

Separation, illness, pre-occupation, all too easily cause a breakdown in communication between parent and child or between spouses which sets up a cumulative chain of distress necessitating a call for help often some long time after the precipitating factor. Recognition of this enables the thread of continuity of goodwill to be found again with mutually beneficent effect. This was true for the Finches.

Mrs Finch referred herself with encouragement from a friend who herself had had help from the clinic and who had observed that Mrs Finch and her 9-year-old son were unresponsive to each other. From the start, Mrs Finch was quite explicit that she was finding it difficult to be a mother to Bob; he is shy, diffident and untruthful and she feels uneasy and unable to approach him. Mother, who has been separated from father for six years, has spent very little time with Bob. When he was born, she felt unable to cope and father took over the baby care and then, when he was 8 months old, Bob was placed in a day nursery whilst both parents were studying. Mother was very depressed at this time. By the time Bob was 3, the parents separated and mother did not see him again until he returned to her care when he was 7. She still felt unable to look after him, so he went to live with his maternal grandmother. When we first saw Mrs Finch and Bob, he had been living with his mother for a year. At the moment of referral mother was having to leave the friend with whom she was staying and for the first time ever she would have sole responsibility for her 9-year-old son. She felt that she did not know anything about boys, that she couldn't talk to her son and he could not talk to her. They needed help to communicate with one another. Mother and Bob were offered six joint meetings which on Bob's initiative were later extended to nine. The first follow-up took place after two months at the worker's suggestion, then mother asked for termly follow-ups for at least a year.

For the most part, work with Bob and his mother was slow, sticky and extremely painful. The worker was faced with a mother and son who had possibly never stayed together for so long. Bob had never been able to express his angry and puzzled feelings about why he could not be closer to the people who were most important to him—his father, his mother and his grandmother—as he put it, 'I want to come here so that mum and I can get to know one another.' Because mother thought that the loss of contact with important people was unavoidable, she had been unable to try to understand and share Bob's feelings. They had never been able to respond to each other emotionally and yet there was still a shred of hope that they could find each other and so they came unfailingly for their appointments and slowly and with great difficulty began to talk to each other about what they felt and thought. In the first meeting, Bob cut out a pattern in coloured paper which remained in his box untouched until the final meeting, when he took it out again, cut out another tiny piece, slightly changing the pattern. He seemed to be saying that the old pattern could be changed a little bit over time, but already a complex pattern had been shaped. One day, after a session, the worker passed them in the street. Bob was skipping beside his mother, his hand in hers. With encouragement, they were able to talk to each other outside the sessions and in the sessions they were able to share with the worker the decisions about the extended contract and about the follow-ups. They learned to tolerate being with each other in the same room, not having to talk, and they began to be sensitive to each other's non-verbal cues. The worker felt that by having extremely limited goals, and a limited commitment with the possibility of future contact, was less frightening to Mrs Finch than an open-ended commitment because she already felt such a failure in open-ended relationships. For Bob and his mother to build any kind of relationship will be slow and difficult and they will probably need intermittent help over a long period through follow-ups and possibly by concentrated pieces of work when they get really stuck. In her work with mother and Bob, the worker had to bear the terrible yawning emptiness, and to persist, in the face of terrible despair and anger, to try to understand what was happening. The sharing of responsibility through reviewing became a model which mother and son began to use at home.

The categories I have described are not an exhaustive list of indications and opportunities for brief focal intervention but do adequately summarize our experience to date. In the next chapter I shall try to identify the techniques and strategies that we have used and the principles underlying their application. Then, in chapter four, I shall examine again how the core values that inform our professional skill interact at every stage with the extension of that skill through each worker's life-span and in relation to the period in which we live.

Chapter three

The dangers of technical know-how without know-why

The teaching and learning of techniques is satisfyingly demonstrable. The process of partializing a task into units that can be completed and which thereby gain an autonomous value, easily divorced from the overall purpose of the exercise, is highly seductive. We have only to look at the attractive simplicity of closed theories of any kind. A few years ago, a consumer magazine reported that oil was the cheapest fuel for central heating. The statement was true at the time and made in good faith but it ignored even the short-term effects of making such a statement. It assumed as given the possibility that all readers had a right to hope for the comforts of central heating and a higher standard of living without computing the ecological, political or economic limitations that are inherent in value choices. If social workers are to develop professional judgment, the application of techniques, which can indeed be learned and helpfully applied, must always be based on expressed values and subject to review in relation to the total context. The context includes new information and understanding generally available, further integration of knowledge and experience in the social worker and the value system of the client and his culture.

The techniques which we have found useful are only appropriate if they *are* appropriate; they are not prescriptions to be randomly applied, even though our experience to date indicates a fairly wide range of applicability. These are:

Mobilizing the coping, adult part of the client

We have seen that in the Millen case (p. 18) this supported the adequate functioning of a group of people with proven potential for filling the roles 'client', 'patient', 'dependant', 'problem'. Many clients who present at a clinic for children and parents cannot be considered as individual casualties. The need to prevent the cycle of deprivation from continuing means that it is unrealistic to concentrate care on one member of a family. Society struggling against odds to compensate for some of the historical misfortunes of a parent, in a way which adversely affects currently dependent children, is a self-defeating operation. On the other hand, if we overvalue the coping adult part of all clients, we deny them the possibility of permission to regress and to acknowledge the infantile parts of themselves within the limits of a secure relationship which may be pre-requisites for very possible and desirable further growth. This is particularly true for clients facing stress from any developmental or accidental crisis. Our own and our clients' sense of a personal continuity that survives pressures, deprivations or persecutions from the environment, that is not a victim of circumstance, is the core of any sense of identity and autonomy. Growth is only possible on a basis of continuity. Sudden ruptures can only be healthily bridged if the links with the past are found again.

Quick take-up

However a client comes to a social worker, the moment of referral is probably the most significant in the whole contact. Who referred or who originated the referral? Who is the client? Whose is the crisis? Why now? Time spent exploring the answers to these questions is well spent. We may all have experience of cases which confirm certain theories which then become a convenient snap judgment. The judgment as to whether the immediate reaction is appropriate in *this* case or whether there are other factors also operating which must be taken into account is the essence of a professional response. It is very necessary to remember that if the 'client' in reality is the referrer and *not* the nominated client, this is not an excuse for neglecting an opportunity for fruitful clarification between agency and referrer which, if not done, is the occasion of the creation of a pseudo-client—of such are many a case-load compounded. None of this alters the fact that the moment of referral is the moment of opportunity. We all know that waiting lists are wonderful devices for making problems disappear, but it is perhaps more useful to know that many a problem fully and promptly explored ceases to be a problem because the resources of the client himself are mobilized and this experience of clarifying and reviewing a situation and choosing the best of available options becomes a model which the client can use again, perhaps without recourse to professional help. The hapless 'waiting list' client, on the other hand, has time to refer himself to other possible sources of help, to develop mistrust of all society's helping organizations or to take panic decisions which convert a temporary dilemma into a chronic problem. If wait there must be, let it be by consent after an initial exploration.

Balance between scientific thinking and 'staying where the client is'

The whole history of social work has wavered between these two extremes. In the early American casework literature there were two opposing schools of thought—the diagnostic and the functional. One laid stress on the collection of historical data and on the classificatory expertise of the professional, the other threw this overboard and concentrated on following the client's here and now, verbalizing observation and restating in a clarifying way what the current concern seemed to be about. We are now more reluctant to throw out the baby with the bath water and struggle to retain scientific detachment and ability to think about the person and the problem in relation to other persons and problems while respecting to a very high degree the individual's uniqueness and the never-before quality of the encounter between this particular client or family at this moment in their life experience and this particular worker at this point in his professional development. It is no easy task to avoid the pitfalls of over-valuation of the professional contribution on the one hand or of the client's autonomy on the other. How is one to strike the right balance between the past and the 'here and now', between useful structure and the maximizing of potential only possible in a situation of flexible refusal to foreclose? In practice, it is always easier to fall back on one extreme or the other—to feel that labelling is a reason for not trying to do anything and is sufficient explanation for the failure of any therapeutic endeavour. This is the hard-headed, man-of-the-world approach. The other extreme, on the whole more common but equally deplorable, is the confused sentimentality of believing that *any*one is capable of *any*thing if only the social worker believes in him, is skilful enough and never succumbs to human failing. Usually this position is sustained by extensive blaming of society's other institutions: social security regulations, education's failings, local unemployment, housing shortage, etc.—anything to protect the image of the kind, good social worker, who never takes a stand, never confronts. It seems to me that a more reasonable and honest middle way requires us to experience more clearly the boundaries around ourselves, our (revisable) diagnostic thinking, our observation and interpretation of the client's behaviour and the boundaries around the client—*his* problem, *his* resources, *his* style; requires us to express this from time to time to check out the perceptions or misperceptions of both parties. The Banks case below illustrates this and also the fourth strategy.

25

Collaboration between the team and between the network of organizations involved

We have alluded to the convenience for the social worker or the client of scapegoating other institutions. Where several agencies or institutions are appropriately involved, they have to reach a series of consensi about consistent strategies and changing emphases if they are not to play ducks and drakes with the taxpayer's money and the unfortunate client's diminished resources. This requires forward thinking and revisable prediction. The forward thinking relates to the agency's responsibility for policy changes, which can only appropriately be made on the basis of a review of past experience; the revisable prediction relates to the outcome of the client's present problem/resources balance and to the relevance of this for future developmental crises so that all possible 'preventive' components can be built into the strategy. The diminution of scapegoating and the increase of rewarding collaboration between agencies will yield future benefits but is never achieved once and for all any more than our own or our client's problems are resolved once and for all, but life would be dull without endeavour. It is worth noting that having a co-worker in one's own or another agency does involve relinquishing something of one's own skill and autonomy, but if the workers can allow each other their respective identities, instead of merging into a sort of brand image, the rewards are sometimes impressive.

Mrs Banks, an attractive, gypsy-looking woman in her early forties, and a single parent, contacted the clinic before Easter for help in the management of her 14-year-old son whose behaviour she was finding uncontrollable and intolerable. Martin refused to let her out of his sight, yelled obscenities at her, and followed her to her evening job as manageress of a restaurant. After dreaming one night that she had tried to murder him, she found herself strangling him the next day, only to be stopped by her sister and mother who were present.

A series of three conjoint exploratory meetings were offered to Mrs Banks by a social worker and a psychiatrist, to be reviewed after the Easter break. Throughout the sessions Martin refused to speak, in fact sat with his eyes closed. Following the sessions he accused his mother of lying and became more unmanageable than before.

During the Easter break (and before the review meeting), Mrs Banks 'phoned the social worker in a state of crisis—she was threatening to harm or to desert Martin and wanted him to be received into care. As the clinic social worker did not have resources to do that, she suggested she accompany Mrs Banks to the nearest area office of the social services department where they were seen immediately by the intake social worker who heard the situation and offered to become involved with Mrs Banks and Martin to assess the problem to see what action might be indicated. Mrs Banks preferred to work with the social services department and not the clinic so it was agreed and arranged that the social services department would take over the case.

After two months of failed appointments and unsuccessful work and a series of continuing crises the social services department social worker re-contacted the clinic social worker for consultation. The two of them with their relevant professional colleagues discussed the case at a workshop and decided to work conjointly with Mrs Banks in her home in an attempt to sort out what past events lay behind some of the management problems she was continuing to have with Martin. The school and the family doctor were concerned and most anxious that something should be done with Martin straightaway.

Three home visits followed by review meetings were offered the mother without Martin and these she accepted willingly. During the visits Martin's behaviour improved as Mrs Banks began to relate her past history of abandonment by her mother at age 2, into care of paternal grandmother, followed by war evacuation to a foster family until aged 14 when she ran away, then contracted TB and was two years in hospital. She married, unhappily, had three children; her beloved grandmother died, her husband left her and she raised Martin and her daughter alone, her eldest son living with Mr Banks. Two years ago she ended an unhappy relationship with a younger man whom Martin had adored. Recently the mother who rejected her came to live nearby and her cherished dog died, because, she felt, of her neglect.

While the two social workers were listening to Mrs Banks' past history and attempting to make links for her between past and present, the situation between Martin and Mrs Banks improved but when the social workers confronted Mrs Banks with her handling of Martin and faced her with her responsibility for her part in his behaviour problem she became angry and annoyed, broke off contact and involved her family doctor by getting him to call the two agency social workers to ask for immediate action and something to be done to have Martin taken into care.

The social workers and doctor met on an emergency basis to try and look at what was going on, what had been accomplished and to establish some forward thinking. The doctor had known Mrs Banks for many years and felt she retreated to physical illness when anxious and under stress. He agreed to support her in continuing to work on *her* problems with Martin. Mrs Banks was informed of this collaborative meeting and the plan for the network to work together co-operatively was communicated to her. She asked for, and was offered, a further series of meetings which she subsequently cancelled. This was taken by the network as an indication that she was at the present moment asking for termination and so the case was closed conjointly by the two agencies and letters were sent to Mrs Banks and to the doctor informing them of the action taken and the reason for the decision with the option to become re-involved if necessary at a future date.

Three months later nothing more had been heard from Mrs Banks. The school was having a problem with Martin's attendance at the beginning of term but they seemed to have coped with him themselves.

Fourteen months later we received a request for a court report for a prosecution re non-attendance at school. Martin resumed attendance while waiting for the court adjournment so the court re-adjourned in the hope of holding the situation till he was due to leave school in a few months. On hearing this Mrs Banks rang the new local authority social worker in tears to say it was not really Martin who was the problem it was she who was upset about the break up of a relationship with a man friend. Society, represented first by the clinic, family doctor and social services department, and later by school, social services department, clinic and court seems to have 'held' this family well enough to enable them to confront their real problems with a consequent reduction in acting-out-by-attribution and wastage of expensive resources.

Therapeutic assessment

Many parents instinctively know that only they can find the right way to respond to their child's problem. Only they know the full complexity and the balance of fact and feeling. They will, however, express a wish for expert advice, for general laws that will somehow reduce their individual pain to a shared, common fact of life for which there is ritualized relief. How ambivalent they feel about this is demonstrated by their indignation at any assumption that they are just like any other Tom, Dick or Harry. We do have the role at times of passer-on of others' resolutions of similar problems—information that can be taken or left, but often it is more appropriate to share with a family what our experience of *them* is. If the initial interview, responding to the referral, is not enough to enable parents or family to cope without further help, in our experience it is more common that neither they nor we are yet in a position to choose an appropriate mode of proceeding further than that the needs and resources are already perceived by both sides to be so clear and complementary that plans for treatment can be agreed forthwith. When this latter happens, as it does sometimes, there is a beginning phase of treatment in which assessment forms an important focus.

Conversely when the understanding of the problem and the resources is still marginal, we have found it very rewarding to stay with the uncertainty through a slow ongoing assessment phase which turns out to have an important therapeutic spin-off.

We often offer a series of assessment interviews (including psychological testing and feedback) which will proceed only until a decision can be made about appropriate termination or treatment. The Norris family already described (p. 17) whose situation was complicated by additional problems not directly connected with the loss were one of these. Such a practice enhances the job satisfaction for the psychologist and the social worker and makes the decision to proceed to a psychiatric assessment a decision shared with the client(s). This can avoid unnecessary use of psychiatric time; it can also avoid the premature withdrawal or prolonged defensiveness of clients whose real or imagined experience of psychiatry is very negative. Family response to the feedback of disinterested observation and speculation about interviews and test responses is often more illuminating than the professionals' contributions *per se*. Children who are implicitly given permission to comment on the interaction in the family from their different standpoints, confirming or modifying the experience in the here and now of the clinic, can and do put their finger on the problem with sureness and in a way which can be made use of by all concerned, and this model of real communication across the generations is something which is henceforward built into the family history and potential repertoire.

The recurrent crisis model

When clients who, in our opinion, have been helped (as far as they were able and as well as we knew how in all the circumstances) return with a new problem, we have to decide whether what was done was wrongly thought out and inadequate or whether what was done was right enough to make them return with greater hope when a new problem arises. At least if they return they have not thought so badly of us that they never want to darken our doors again. In the last year, 10 per cent of our cases returned with another problem. For some of these we had predicted that this was to be expected. From their previous use and experience of helping agencies we recognized that only a diminution of need or a briefer use of help would indicate progress. Others we had no reason to expect to return and we were glad that the break in contact enabled us to re-assess the current needs, without the shadow of the past pattern of response setting the expectations on both sides in one fixed dimension. The Anderson family (see p. 12) and another parent used the clinic resources in a much more peripheral and autonomous way the second time round. It was as though they were asking not for help this time, but for confirmation that we did not wish to revoke the confidence in their coping potential that we had previously conveyed.

Nine months after their first contact, Mrs Anderson approached the clinic for help with Jeremy who was school refusing. An appointment was offered the parents and Jeremy but only mother and son attended. Mrs Anderson stated clearly her desire for Jeremy to come for treatment for himself. Jeremy refused saying he would prefer to go back to school if only he could be excused from physical education and drama. The problem was felt to be between the Andersons and Jeremy and the school, which Mrs Anderson was going to explore with the education welfare officer and be back in touch.

Although nothing more was heard directly from the Andersons, soon the education welfare officer 'phoned asking for reports and help for the school in dealing with the recurrent school crisis. Based on previous experience of the Andersons' ability to cope with problems on their own if given encouragement and the knowledge of Jeremy's recent refusal of help for himself, the clinic social worker suggested a meeting at school which might include herself, the Andersons and all the school staff concerned. She offered to inform the Andersons of the school's concern and request for help and to invite them to the meeting. The school agreed in principle to the meeting but queried the wisdom of the parents and child being included. The compromise reached was that only the parents would be invited. The school was aware that the Andersons had ended their contact with the clinic a year ago and were reluctant to become re-involved. They accepted the challenge of the problem with Jeremy being now their problem and with the clinic support were prepared to become engaged with the parents in attempting to work out a mutually acceptable solution.

The clinic social worker felt her role in the school meeting to be that of enabler, and anticipated using herself and her interventions in a limited and focused way so that both the school and parents might address themselves to the task in hand and resolve their problems.

The school meeting lasted an hour and went through three distinct phases. The first phase involved both school and parents taking up defensive positions, each feeling it was the other's fault (and each blaming the other). The second phase was more task-orientated with the school taking the lead and sharing with the parents their genuine interest in Jeremy as pupil and their wish to know how best to help him. The third phase was a mutual engagement of the parents and school together in attempting to find solutions and resolutions to Jeremy's present and expressed school difficulties. The clinic social worker's conscious and planned use of herself through her appropriately placed comments and questions enabled the parties concerned to reach amicable, workable and acceptable solutions to the problems at hand.

The result was that the school felt a relieved sense of achievement, as did the parents. The parents acknowledged the help given them by saying they no longer felt there was a need for Jeremy to return to the clinic. The school, on the other hand, asked if more help could be given to them in the future by the clinic, for they had many difficulties with other children. At this moment, the school felt both pride and satisfaction that they had dealt successfully with one very difficult and persistent problem.

What is the minimum we need do?

This confidence in the client's resources makes it important to ask ourselves this question. We are not in business to demonstrate how good we are at doing things for people, whether for clients or in order to provide statistics or busy-ness for employers. Because the question may also carry a connotation of laziness or contempt for unworthy clients, it is sometimes easier not to ask it. The fact is that it is much harder work thinking rigorously before we act and resisting the temptation to infantilize the client instead of tacitly expecting his collaboration. Sometimes it is easier to convey confidence in their resources to clients far removed from our own social or professional status than to those whose dilemma feels much nearer home. The Inez family illustrate many aspects of brief focal work including this one.

Mr Inez, here with his family on a sabbatical year from a South American university was studying at the postgraduate school associated with the clinic. The social worker and psychologist who agreed to take on the case were the only staff available who did not already know Mr Inez and his family. Mr Inez and his wife were finding their 13-year-old son, Kenneth's, adjustment to England increasingly disturbing. They had been here six months and felt that was time enough for him to settle in as had they and their 6-year-old daughter. On the contrary, Kenneth had become more and more upset and miserable, having no friends, complaining constantly and finding fault with everyone and everything at the school. He was also suffering from bowel retention.

Two exploratory interviews were offered by the social worker to the parents who came on the first occasion without Kenneth, and on the second brought him as he was so distressed at school. Kenneth begged someone to do something—he felt completely hopeless but decided with his parents that one way to begin might be with psychological tests so that he could at least see how he compared with other children of his age in England as he was finding all of his classes so confusing.

The testing took three sessions during which time the parents chose *not* to meet with the social worker as they felt they had nothing more to say and the only one with problems was Kenneth. They had revealed in their first session that Kenneth's problems had been evident back home and his school there had arranged that he see a psychiatrist who recommended analysis for him because of the degree of his disturbance. The parents had not seen the need for this and decided to postpone doing anything until after their sabbatical year in hopes that he would outgrow it. Mr Inez disclosed that he himself was currently in therapy as he found himself experiencing a mid-life career crisis and felt unable to cope with any problems Kenneth might be having. Mrs Inez was counting the days until she returned home.

The psychological tests revealed an extremely bright boy who had deep-seated problems that would be best treated by long-term intensive therapy. Because of the disturbing nature of the test results and Kenneth's lack of communication with his parents, the parents and Kenneth were offered a series of four meetings in which to discuss these results and the implications for the future for, because of the degree of Kenneth's disturbance, it was felt to be inappropriate for the clinic to offer treatment as the recommendation was for long-term psychotherapy, anything else being contra-indicated. The parents were angry with the clinic for making a recommendation for treatment yet being unwilling to provide anything and attempted to bring pressure to bear via their friends within the clinic. The team resisted the pressures, assured by their colleagues that the stand they had taken was in the child's and parents' best interests. Kenneth himself agreed with the test opinion by confirming that his problems were so severe it would take at least two years before he could ever trust anyone enough to begin to talk about the things that bothered him.

The parents' anger with the team was relentless. They felt incapable of dealing with their son and wanted help but when offered the opportunity of sessions on their own to explore ways *they* might better deal with Kenneth they refused. For the last session the father came alone. He announced that he and his wife were struggling to make a decision to arrange therapy for Kenneth when they returned home in six months, yet knew that finances would be a problem as he (father) was in the process of changing careers. He also revealed a past history of marital disharmony punctuated by frequent separations.

Mr Inez was asked if he and his wife would like a further meeting in a month's time and this time he accepted. When they returned they felt more confident and organized.

They had begun to make enquiries at home about a therapist for Kenneth which they found had helped to reassure Kenneth and to alleviate their anxiety. They asked about the advisability of help for themselves as a couple and a family which they were encouraged to pursue. Mr Inez had decided definitely to postpone his career decision for at least several years until after his son and the family were settled. They acknowledged the help given them, that decisions had been made and that changes had occurred within the family, but they wanted us to know that, given their choice, they would have preferred the clinic to have treated Kenneth and not to have left everything to them to arrange.

If I have described strategies rather than techniques or tactics, it is, I think, because like most social workers I have a profound respect for individual differences in clients and in workers. One cannot acquire judgment by applying rules uncritically; professional workers cannot escape responsibility for taking decisions about why this method now. Habit, tradition in the agency or the latest textbook recipe are not good enough so we are forced back once more to examine the values that permeate our decisions. In the next chapter I shall look again at how we learn from experience.

Chapter four

Learning from experience

The client's self-image: reality-testing

Sir Geoffrey Vickers (1972), writing about the challenges facing our civilization, wrote, 'The judgment of men by men is the proper business of men. The appreciative world in which we live is peopled by our appreciations of each other.' Earlier formulations (Rogers, 1951) about how casework worked often alluded to the value for the client of the worker reflecting back the statements and feeling-tone the client was expressing so that he could recognize and explore them further. The concept implied a relatively inactive role for the social worker, and, as a technical exercise for the naturally overactive, it has its value, but I suspect that sometimes our real self, rather than some professional mirror self, is of real service to our clients. Statements like 'It seems to me that you (father) are carrying all the disciplinary and outer-world expectations part of parenting and you (mother) are carrying all the understanding, excusing, extenuating side of parenting and that perhaps neither can be wholly right and perhaps both of you would sometimes like to exchange roles?' are not only a private reflecting-back, they are also realistic feedback. For many people who have imperfectly surmounted their own identity crisis, who feel obscurely that they play roles in a fraudulent way rather than feel certain who they are in a variety of circumstances, the experience of feedback is growth promoting and when life circumstances fail to provide enough of this experience, this component in the therapeutic situation may be crucial.

We have to confront our clients with reality even though we recognize the validity of their feeling. For example, if a husband feels that he had a vasectomy to please his wife and his wife feels that it was a joint decision after four years of trying alternative methods after the pill had been found unsuitable for her, it is relevant both to reflect back one's recognition that both feelings are valid to the person expressing them *and* to allude to the fact that, explicit or not, a decision was taken and acted on that it was husband, not wife, who would be sterilized.

In trying to formulate more accurately what elements are involved in the worker's progressive appreciation of the client and his exercise of judgment about the evidence before him, it seems to me first, that the worker's ability to recognize and voice what the client is on the verge of knowing consciously himself is important and second, that while preserving his own integrity, the worker must be 'in it' with the client, trying to preserve a marriage of feeling and thought and using empathic understanding in order to offer tentative explanatory interpretations or conceptual links which may enable the client to make sense of his experience. The response of the client to these efforts by the worker either corroborates the accuracy of the formulation or calls for an improved approximation—and so the process of reality-testing proceeds, both client and worker learning in the process. For the client, the experience of someone else struggling to perceive him and his situation accurately and prepared to offer the evidence of his eyes and ears for their joint consideration, gives a rare opportunity for the adult part of himself to make an alliance with the helper to look at, think about and understand the more infantile and conflict-ridden parts of himself and so to be able to make his own choices and decisions on the basis of a clearer map of his circumstances.

Review: thinking about what, why and how, reviewing with the client, task-setting

I would like to explore the concept of review as a tool for learning from experience. One of the advantages of working in a teaching clinic is the sanction to take time to think with students about all the information one has at any, but particularly the first, stage of contact with a case. That this stopping and thinking leads to economical use of time should be reason enough for non-teaching practitioners also to feel sanctioned to review information before action. We have discussed the paramount importance for the client of the moment of referral. For the worker, that first encounter is crucial for the development of an appropriate strategy. Rather than feeling, as is all too easy, that action should be delayed until more information is available, we do well to think about the information we do have: written communications, behaviour, verbal and non-verbal communications. If our perceptors are fully alert, we probably have available, very early on, a miniaturized 'snap' of which subsequent meetings will only serve as enlargements. What is the problem, why now, and how may this client be able to resolve it are proper questions to ask if one is bent on making the minimum necessary intervention and on learning all one can from the experience of the first encounter. Just as many clients (and many social workers too!) have never had enough feedback of how other people perceive them, many have had little experience of reviewing their life-pattern development, and the active participation of the client in reviewing his own behaviour in the present in relation to how he has behaved in other situations in the past, can bring back choice into a situation which is intolerable because of the apparent absence of choice. One may not be able to alter circumstances, one may be able to do something about managing oneself vis-à-vis the circumstances. Better ways of responding may well need both practice (before they become built-in) and opportunities to test out whether attempts have been successful or not. Review, therefore, leads to mutually agreed task-setting and follow-up. Bob and his mother (see p. 21) are a good example of this. The social worker's responsibility for the management of time by spacing contact is an important part of the client's acquiral or resumption of autonomy. A research currently being undertaken by Silove (1976) into the needs and aspirations of social workers pursuing post-professional education indicates already that some of the most crucial questions facing them are about confrontation and time-management. Working in bureaucracies where it is often not clear where bucks do stop, and where pressures of work can be felt to be overwhelming, where does the social worker cry halt? Is it better to have a high incidence of sick leave and a high staff turnover rate or to utilize study leave purposefully at all points in the hierarchy? If, for the client, the experience of reviewing his behaviour patterns makes it possible to take a different turn the next time round, the social worker involved with the problems of x clients can similarly feel trapped into habitual maladaptive responses and in need of time to review possible alternatives. It is not as though there is one sure formula which, once learnt, makes the rest of professional life smooth-running. We cannot avoid pain and imperfect resources but we can learn cumulatively from our experience, if we call a halt in order to review our experience and to define our legitimate individual boundaries and the negotiations that are required for transactions across those boundaries. We use the feelings engendered in us by clients and colleagues to help us understand their situation. Unless we have some notion of what is us and what is them, we feel invaded, persecuted, or influenced by them and thereby the less a free agent, who can select an appropriate response. How do we manage our own boundaries so that on the one hand they do not have such massive defences that coming and going across the boundary has the quality of a battle operation or, on the other, that we almost wonder whether 'we' really exist or whether all the traffic is not the only thing that other people think is real? If we have these feelings, although their intensity will vary from one situation to another, we need to find out what helps us to cope with them if we are to convey to clients, who are feeling incapacitated by circumstances, that it is possible to learn from experience by reviewing one's responses and by defining one's boundaries and accepting some responsibility for what goes on within them. Our sense of our own identity and boundaries is enhanced by radar-like soundings off our environment and for this our environment must be sufficiently containing—you do not get echoes if there are no walls for sound to bounce back from. The containment may vary on a dimension from embracing arms to prison walls but, for purposes of identity definition, either is more effective than indifference. Urban anomie is as unsustaining to social workers as it is to clients, so it behoves us to think well about how we manage ourselves and our own stresses if we are to be able to help clients as opposed to going through the motions of helping. In the long run it is only in so far as we keep on growing ourselves that we can help our clients to do that.

The importance of the experience of continuity

Just as life in the biological organism depends on the continuity of essential functions through injury or disease in spite of pain and limitation, so psychic life and health depends on the maintenance of an essential continuity of experience.

Tyhurst (1957) relating the development of mental illness to experience of transitional states, including disasters, considered that discontinuity is a major causative factor. Where people undergoing sudden change of circumstances can be encouraged to talk and to link their previous with their present state without being removed from their current circumstances (by e.g. hospitalization) the outlook for eventual successful resolution of the crisis is high. Where further discontinuities are recommended in the name of 'help', the outlook is much graver. The experience of important discontinuities in infancy through child-placing activity is so familiar in the history of adults with difficulties that we become defeatist about the possibility of retrieving the thread of experience. Allowing clients to talk with feeling about past traumas when they are re-evoked by present experiences is one of the opportunities we do have to intervene 'preventively' in relation to the future. In terms of focus in our work, perhaps continuity of experience, this simple criterion for growth, is more important than anything else. Winnicott (1971a) has described with immense sensitivity how much one single intervention along the lines of finding again the continuities of experience can re-open a child's potential for maturation. Both the Norrises (see p. 17) and the Bankses (see p. 26), cited in the previous two chapters, illustrate the release of coping capacity that occurs when past painful experiences can be integrated to the present sense of a continuing self instead of having to be cut off or kept at bay by heavy psychic expenditure. Marris's work (1974) takes this theme to a very valuable higher level of abstraction so that the theoretical links between the management of mourning loss by death and the management of the loss involved unavoidably in change and innovation can be applied in a rich variety of situations.

For the professional worker, the ability to relate to the client's continuity depends very greatly on his own constantly renewed ability to be in touch with his own experience at all periods of his life. How does one remain supple and able to acknowledge the painful developmental struggles one has been through oneself? Hard-won adult behaviour so often seems to be achieved at the cost of suppressing the memory of the helplessness, the envy, jealousy, anger and loving of childhood. We ignore at our peril the fact that if we alienate ourselves from our own roots, including both the painful and pleasant emotions, we also alienate ourselves from our creative potential, our ability to respond with a 'never before' spontaneity and appropriateness to the unique individuals who present to us.

What all the case illustrations you have read in the preceding two chapters could be said to have in common is the fact that the attention of the professional workers enabled the people concerned to find thinking and feeling space to work out the best option open to them, to learn something valuable from their own experience. How do we develop our capacity to attend to another's situation? Attention implies an ability to stay with the chaos and pain and uncertainty, and that staying power is only possible if we have an inner conviction, born out of our own experience, that this is a rewarding pattern of behaviour. Social workers are not automatically endowed with all the wisdom of experience on qualification. How dull it would be if there were not new learning to take place throughout life, but somehow, we have to acquire a model of attention, of concentration on and empathy with another's experience. The scientific discipline of observation, recording and retrospective making sense of experience is enormously relevant here. The capacity to observe and remember another's reality without stereotyping or moralizing is a pre-requisite for new understanding. To appreciate another's reality requires mental space to allow the mind to play around alternative constructions, requires the emotion to be recollected in tranquillity if the contribution of the professional is to be genuinely relevant.

Social workers tend to under-value their skills. We need to own our unacceptable feelings but we need no less to own our skills in knowing when to be active, when to be inactive, when our attention is potent, when to share our imperfect understanding.

Much of what I have written may be viewed as a translation for today of social work writing of many decades past. I make no apology for this. Every generation has to learn for itself, every individual has to learn and re-learn throughout life and the task of pushing out the boundaries of learning while remaining in touch with the core values is what integrity is about.

It seems to me less important to popularize a fashionable method than to foster an attitude which enables flexibility in functioning and, above all, the exercise of judgment. Social workers and other professionals are impeded from commitment to appropriate professional goals and from genuine and necessary involvement and engagement with clients by internal and external factors. If the present book helps us in any way to own our respective responsibility for understanding and reviewing the internal factors, this knowledge will be really under our belts and we will be better able to understand the factors that impede our clients from exploring their own reality. When this inside work is clearer and more coherent, the boundaries between inside and outside can be confidently crossed. Social action is indeed more appropriate for some problems than accommodation to unnecessary evils. Social work agency organization can and should be reviewed critically so that it facilitates and supports more than it frustrates and misleads.

Emerging themes

I have tried to convey something of my own metabolism of interchanges with colleagues of different disciplines and agencies whose preoccupations have proved to be similar. I think it is not untrue to claim that we are all struggling to bring together familiar principles into a gestalt that is new for the 1970s. The themes that seem to me to emerge from all the categories of cases, from all the strategies described are fourfold, and, at the risk of repeating myself, I would like to restate them as follows:

Attention

When a teacher says, 'Pay attention!' or a sergeant shouts, ''tenshun!', we have an image of alert concentration on the task in hand. The image is modified when we talk of a nurse attending to a patient's needs or a mother attending to her baby, but in all cases a receptivity to verbal and perhaps more particularly to non-verbal cues is implied. Attention acts as a container within which experience can be digested. When we are preoccupied with other things we cannot attend and similarly within the family, parents preoccupied with their own problems cannot attend to their children helpfully. Social workers too often collude with this and if the 1970s are remembered for nothing else I would like to think that it will prove to be the decade in which more of us developed real conviction about the value of attending to the communications of the children in our case-loads. Our own flight from the pain that children experience will be less necessary if we can allow ourselves to learn humbly from children how they can cope resiliently if our attention enables their situations to be contained long enough to be worked on.

When someone feels trapped in a confused and conflictual situation, being listened to facilitates work on clarifying that situation but it is also too simple to assert that being a good listener is all that is required. Active help with tentative structuring of the situation and making links between past and present experience or present experience in different areas of life is part of the process of being available to clients which is more than an inert receptivity, it is also an engagement to contribute in. Hoxter (1974), in an unpublished paper, has used the phrase 'space in my mind' and this describes very well the important conjunction of 'space' and 'mind'. The helper must be willing to put his mind—intelligence and understanding—at the service of another in struggling to delineate a situation in a way which makes freedom of choice possible where only painful conflict was experienced before.

I am aware that, in trying to make awareness of the unconscious operating more available to social workers, who for the most part will not have been analysed nor have experienced therapy for themselves, I run the risk of seeming to recommend either an unacceptable dilution of established knowledge (to the analytically experienced) or an over-confident assumption that stretches the credulity of the unsophisticated or theoretically antagonistic. Nevertheless, since Thackeray could describe the reactions of the Viscountess Castlewood (in *Henry Esmond*) to the sudden death of her husband in a way which would have corroborated in detail the later scientific formulations about the processes of loss and mourning and since many of the initially shocking insights, for the first time scientifically expressed by Freud as opposed to being intuitively known by writers and artists, have become very widely acknowledged in our society, it would be presumptuous to underestimate the degree of available self-knowledge and freedom to observe what is under one's nose which may be present in anyone whose work demands some effort of understanding of others. I think the worker's struggle to make sense for himself of what clients bring to him is effective only if it draws him closer to the clients and their struggle to make sense of their experiences. Hence, both workers and clients are engaged in a process of using their pre-conscious knowledge in the service of explanation. It feels impossible to fight an unknown enemy. The discomfort of chaos and uncertainty is painful for worker and client and the struggle to bear this until some meaningful conceptual links can be made is only possible if the worker's hopefulness survives the client's experience of despair.

Continuity

The theme of continuity recurs again and again: an individual's continuity from his roots in infancy; what he goes on making of his cumulative experience; how past events reverberate in the present; how present help can be relevant for the future, however deprived or pathological the past. Professional helpers need to be in touch with their own continuity, their past, their potential for the future if they are to enter imaginatively and with enough courage into another's reality. Their sense of historical process in groups and communities has to span past and future in terms of understanding how the past has influenced the present and how inevitable change, and the loss that this involves, can be negotiated without loss of continuity. There is enormous skill involved in helpful intervention. The exercise of judgment in deciding what and when and why is not magically acquired, neither is it nothing more than the common touch. If we increase our range of effectiveness even a little each year of our professional life, it is no small achievement in our own continuum. Let us acknowledge our limitations but let us also value our skills, which we have a responsibility to articulate and to make teachable to other disciplines.

Paradoxes and judgment

The third theme is harder to express pithily but I suppose the *holding of opposites* is as near as I can get to it. The notion of ambivalence has been around long enough for most people to have at least an intellectual understanding that it is possible to feel two ways about something at the same time; similarly, the notion that all is rarely black or white but more often grey attracts lip service but I am after something more widely relative. There is a difference between perceiving something in focus at a given point on a dimension and perceiving simultaneously also what is out of focus at both ends of the dimension. How do we attend to the child in the adult, to the adult in the child? How do we decide when to initiate a discussion that we sense will be relevant and when to suspend judgment and follow what the client brings? Why must we remember

41

both the strengths and the weaknesses of our clients and ourselves? Why did the worker decide that the label of school refuser for Jeremy Anderson (see p. 13) did not call for a stereotyped response or despair on the part of the worker? What governs our choice of individual or group as the unit of attention? How can one push out the professional boundaries and remain in touch with the base-camp core values?

The approach I have described is full of paradoxes. One experienced clinician experienced using brief focal strategies as paradoxically giving people more time. One colleague asked why we had not included a failure in the illustrations and when we reviewed the entire two years' work we felt that all the cases demonstrated both failure and success in a way that made the terms irrelevant or presumptuous.

I realize as I write about paradoxes how much my thinking about the inescapable subtleties of work has been enriched by Winnicott's (1971b) expression of the process by which the infant both discovers and creates reality. Maybe if infants can manage paradoxes, we, in our better moments, can glimpse them too!

Recognition and affirmation

Educationists are familiar with notions of reinforcement and positive feedback. Therapists perhaps tend to take acceptance of the client for granted and stress in fact the alertness necessary to perceive when the client is inviting one to collude or is somehow running rings round one. We have talked earlier about the helpful experience for the client that having himself and his problem recognized constitutes. It is just as important, it seems to me, for the client to feel that his efforts and achievements are recognized and affirmed. Not only because nothing succeeds like success but because permission to grow and achieve is a very proper communication from a representative of society to an individual member.

A further question, about how many cases a given worker can carry in this way, deserves attention. All the staff and trainees concerned had diversified case-loads on other programmes as well as the brief focal programme. They all attended a weekly or fortnightly workshop of one and a half hours, they all could have access to a resource person who was not him or herself involved in the case and could help to sort out the counter-transference when the family pathology seemed to get into the team. These institutionalized support systems certainly enabled good work to be done and learning to take place. The flexible approach to work style was mirrored in the flexible use of team collaboration. The learning was certainly not only done by the least experienced. Effective helping requires the containment of pain and a high level of self-management by the worker. I suppose we can be busy giving ineffective help, but I suppose, too, that we can all try to create one area of work in which we and our colleagues move towards greater effectiveness in both skill and agency organization. Either way we will fill the time available. We won't achieve perfection but we can enjoy the journey.

Chapter five

The professional workers' self-management

Professional workers have to exercise judgment not only about clients—but also, in a very major way, about themselves. Who do I work for—myself, my clients or my agency? Where do I stand when there is conflict between professional satisfaction and service productivity?

Does my agency respond to needs, to demands or merely to values and circumstances of an earlier age confusedly perpetuated? What responsibility and capacity do I have for contributing to agency change in a desired direction or for recognizing when that task will be subject to so much frustration that I should not accept or should leave such a post? How much congruence is necessary between the role attributed to me by society and the perceptions of my role by myself and my working group? For example, social work informed with psychoanalytic understanding is criticized in some English circles for working for social conformity at the expense of individual freedom or change and in some American states is prohibited as dangerously subversive.

How we, as individual workers, use time is a matter for our judgment however often we protest about the pressures and requirements of the job. We all have twenty-four hours in a day and what we do with them depends on our judgment of priorities, our ability to keep to time boundaries and our decisions about what we do within those boundaries. Within the time contracted for work for our agency how do we adopt goals that are a challenge to individual and team endeavour yet take into account historical and political realities without being defeated by them? Within the time contracted for the work with a client what is the optimum rigidity or flexibility in relation to the agreed focus? When is it appropriate to encourage dependence, when to affirm autonomy? When is our therapeutic enthusiasm crucial, when is it essential to leave the client to find his own right time to do necessary work? Can we grow in skill without becoming destructively perfectionist—when are our interventions good enough and when are results good enough? In the here and now of the interview can we trust our own unconscious to keep working when our conscious understanding is overwhelmed? Can we trust the patient's capacity to explore his own situation and believe in his potential for growth? Unless we can we will not be able to keep hope alive in the face of the client's despair and unless the content of our own hope is realistic it may still prove to be a delusion. Here again we have to situate ourselves somewhere between total reliance on established theory and total abandonment to unstructured observation. Unless we have some backbone of explanatory theory of proven utility we cannot withstand the impact of distress long enough to hold it in our minds, trying to metabolize it instead of simply reacting against it, but unless we can also abandon theory and allow ourselves to see, trying to make sense of what is under our noses, we cannot hope to extend or link existing theories or develop new ones. For this we need both self-confidence and humility—self-confidence that what we have assimilated and interpreted to date will stand us in good stead even in confusing and frightening new situations and humility to acknowledge that there is more to learn when learning sometimes means unlearning what we think we know.

Where does this leave us in relation to the time much less formally contracted for—time for self, family, friends—time for sleeping? Social workers whose conditions of employment require them to work not a specified number of hours but according to the requirements of the service have a very substantial responsibility to balance the reasonable and unreasonable demands of the service against their own stamina, job and private life-satisfactions. What amount of refreshment away from work actually increases one's efficacy and creativity at work? Is working overtime a disease, a virtue or a matter for fine judgment? What amount of work enriches—financially and in other ways—one's private life? What about the times one dreams—or has nightmares—about work? Certainly if one cannot find time and mental space for metabolizing the psychic pain one encounters in the course of work, if the bombardment of distressing situations comes so thick and fast that one has to sleep before digestion can be done, one will carry that working-over process into one's sleeping time and dreams or nightmares will be part of the continuing effort to deal with the experiences. If one can withhold one's natural indignation at such an invasion of one's night life, the reduced rationality of one's waking moments can be a fertile opportunity for recognizing significant links and increasing understanding. It may, with justice, be said that social work agencies should be so organized that effective support for its social workers under stress is built-in, in office time, but the best organization in the world cannot forestall the possibility that there will be times when work will be carried over into dreams or wakeful periods. If one is so detached from one's work that this never happens one should perhaps ask oneself whether responsibility for such non-involvement rests with oneself or with the particular job. It is hard to imagine either personal or professional growth taking place without involvement.

After time, money is the next major area for discretional judgments. As social workers move up the employment hierarchy they are liable to have to make decisions about discretionary grants for individual cases, about priorities for claims upon a limited budget, about fund raising activities, about financing future planning projects. Does one contribute the drop that may seem to be lost in an ocean of need? Does one refuse traditional claims in favour of a dramatic new cause which may prove to be a lost cause? Does one invest in people or in things? In training or in service? In direct help or to foster self-help? In research or in expansion? In a society that often measures endeavour or success by the amount of money spent how does one budget one's personal influence? If clients tend to get a better deal when staff morale is high, how is morale maintained?— by new buildings and equipment, by staff development programmes, by individualized support and encouragement? At a time when participation is very much an 'in' concept, even the lowliest social worker's responsibility for thinking about his work in terms of value for money is intimately linked with his capacity to value himself and his clients and to seek affirmation for this from time to time.

Management of self means having an opinion about how much handicap/limitation/depression and how much strength/imagination is useful in helping one to identify with clients, how much is too much and what helps to redress the balance; it means knowing what is self and what is other, it means resisting bureaucratization, knowing how to retain both uniqueness and belonging; it means accepting the inevitable relationship between freedom of choice on the one hand and constraint and containment on the other.

In Part II we shall be looking at some case studies and their authors' comments. I have sought to draw on the work of fellow programme-members and of colleagues who have independently reached comparable formulations.

Part two

Corroboration from the experience of others

Chapter six

Brief focal intervention in family mourning: Visha

Elizabeth Tuters

The case

Visha Hill, aged 10, an only child, was referred by her mother to the clinic for school refusing, two and a half months following the death of her father. The mother felt incapable of providing the required help as she was too upset herself. She was planning to leave the country soon and go to her home, Ceylon, to visit her mother and extended family.

A few days after the referral telephone call, they were both seen. Quick pick-up is a tactic highly revered in brief focal work and immediately a team of child psychiatrist (Dr Holland); social worker (Mrs Tuters); and educational psychologist (Mrs Waterfall) was formed. We decided that Dr Holland and Mrs Tuters would first meet mother and child as a foursome to share with them the plan of an exploratory phase of four individual meetings, Visha with Dr Holland and mother with Mrs Tuters.

First contract

Exploratory phase, individual meetings; four sessions once a week

These separate meetings with the two pairs revealed the awfulness of Mrs Hill's and her daughter's experiences. Visha had come home one day from school to find her father lying dead in bed. He had had a chest pain and was being treated for rheumatism; the cause of death was heart attack. Mrs Hill felt guilty and blamed herself for not having insisted that her husband see the doctor again. At the time of death, Mrs Hill and Visha managed efficiently and single handedly all of the necessary funeral arrangements. Now Mrs Hill found herself unable to cope, she was tearful, not sleeping, dreaming of her husband's dead body stretched across her bed, drinking to

49

excess and quarrelling with Visha. She felt she had no communication with Visha who criticised her for being weak and silly and not getting a hold of herself.

Mrs Hill painfully told of an unhappy marriage. Both she and her husband were musicians in their mid-forties, married ten years. She for the first time, he for the second. They married apparently because they believed in the same philosophy of classical music, but after Visha's birth it all changed. Mrs Hill was forced to stay at home with her baby and unable to pursue her career; Mr Hill went out and became involved in more modern music and techniques. Gradually the gap widened so that for the past five years they lived completely separate lives. Mrs Hill in her part of the house, Mr Hill in his. They never even spoke. Visha went in between the two.

Mr and Mrs Hill's own histories were troubled and it was possible to see how their unresolved past conflicts affected their marital relationship.

Mrs Hill was herself an only child in an intellectual Ceylonese family. Her own parents married late, after being well established in their own careers—her father as a colonial administrator and her mother as a headmistress. When Mrs Hill was 4 years old her father died of a heart attack, her mother worked and she was brought up by servants. She feared her mother and saw her as strict, rigid and Victorian. They were never close and only had disagreements. After university, Mrs Hill moved away from her mother to become a music teacher in a girls' school, but found that unsatisfactory and moved back home. Again the relationship with her mother became difficult so she went to England where she met and married Mr Hill. Although their marital relationship had deteriorated, the relationship both she and her husband had with her mother improved. In fact, her mother and husband had become very close and they mutually respected each other. The Hill family had been planning a trip together to Ceylon in the coming year—that was where they had all been happiest five years ago and felt such happiness would be recoverable again. Mr Hill's untimely death shattered the dream—in Mrs Hill's own words, 'I never expected the story to end this way.'

Mr Hill's family history, as given by Mrs Hill, was necessarily incomplete. His parents were living but seemed to feature less significantly. By a previous marriage he had two children, an adolescent boy and girl, who were living with their mother in Spain. The first marriage seemed fraught with tensions and frequent separations and finally dissolved over an adulterous act by the wife with his best friend. This so enraged Mr Hill he demanded a divorce, fully expecting custody of his children, who were awarded to their mother and taken back to the wife's home in Spain to be brought up by their wealthy aristocratic grandparents. Mr Hill pined for his

50

children but could never find the money nor bring himself to visit them, until a few years ago when he went with Visha. It was Mrs Hill's hope that the reunion of her husband with his children would magically provide the key to happiness in their marriage. She felt confident her marriage would never dissolve as she knew her husband would never risk losing his child with whom he was completely involved to the exclusion of almost everyone.

Visha in her individual sessions showed through her drawings, plasticine models and stories how devastated and all alone she felt with no one in the world to help her. Her defence against those overwhelming feelings was to insist on seeing her world as happy, all filled with happy birds and gardens and never ending supplies of ice cream. She concentrated all her energies into being highly critical of her mother's 'tearful carry-on', missing her best school friend and being worried about black spiders that lurk about in unexpected places.

In these sessions we monitored carefully Visha's and Mrs Hill's responses to interpretation and reflective discussion. They both quickly formed positive relationships with us and experienced relief at being able to talk. As mother said, 'You are the first person who let me talk, who listened and tried to understand.' Visha was less in touch with her feelings than her mother, but she was an extremely verbal child, well composed and adult-like in her responses.

As a team we weighed the strengths and resources we saw operating in the two in terms of what we could realistically do together within the time we had available, which was three months. We decided on the basis of our observable evidence that our primary focus would be on strengthening the mother-daughter relationship, *as they had only each other*. Our goal was to try and open up blocked avenues of communication. By helping them to share with us the pain of father's death we hoped to make it possible for them to share their pain with each other and thus re-establish the contact which they seemed to have lost over the years. Our proposed strategy was to meet as a foursome in the clinic with the addition of psychological tests for Visha, who was manifesting school problems in attendance, learning and behaviour.

Second contract

Conjoint meetings, four sessions offered: two cancelled

In the review meeting following the first four sessions this thinking and the plan for conjoint meetings was shared with the Hills and mutually agreed upon. Subsequently, the first conjoint session was cancelled fifteen minutes before time because Visha had an asthma

51

attack. We reasoned that somatization of the conflict was due to our decision to bring the four of us together, thereby bringing mother and daughter, and the already formed pairs, into direct contact in an attempt to deal with the family splits. On the basis of this hypothesis we decided to offer twice weekly sessions for the remaining weeks and this was willingly accepted by the Hills. In the session, Mrs Hill seemed worried and depressed, Visha seemed flat and said she was afraid her mother would start to yell and scream. Visha alarmed us with a cold description of her go-between position in her parents' marriage and with the responsibility she felt for her parents' happiness and now for her mother's mental health. 'I was a shuttlecock, going between the two!' Mrs Hill added sadly, 'She lived in fear of upsetting the peculiar balance.' As the next session was about to begin Mrs Hill rang to say Visha was having another more severe asthma attack.

Crisis

We responded to this attack as a crisis in light of the material revealed in the previous session and offered to make a home visit. It was during this home visit that we got a clearer vision of the mother's strengths and insights which helped us define our focus even more. We were struck by the complete feeling of inadequacy this mother experienced and yet how coping and adequate we found her, for in the face of this severe asthma attack she knew exactly what to do. In fact, she had anticipated the asthma and she herself interpreted this as the way Visha coped with painful feelings. She told us Visha began to have asthma at the same time the parents' relationship began to deteriorate, thereby making a link between the onset of asthma and the parental relationship.

Inside the home we were ourselves overwhelmed with the reality of the father's death. His photographs, music, tapes and records were everywhere. It was as if in a shrine, complete with a tiny vase of fresh flowers by a large portrait. We became aware of memories of the past, their relationship to the present and of the ghost of father that seemed to be holding them together. The impact of this led us to suggest we continue to meet in the home. Mrs Hill thought this was a good idea yet thought that Visha might prefer the clinic—'She likes to get away for a little trip.' We were struck by the parallel of this as exactly what they would be doing in a few weeks.

Third contract

Home visits, two sessions a week for three weeks

When we arrived we found Visha in the sitting room. We explored with her her feelings about the home visits. She felt it was better to meet at home—'I know this place inside out; where every spider lives.'

Visha then told us how her worst fears were now coming true, how she and her mother had a horrible fight and her mother began to scream and yell so that Visha could not stand it and she had run to get help from the new tenants who had moved into her father's bedroom. Visha considered her mother to be very weak. Mother appealed to Visha, saying she was not strong. 'If you really knew what I was then we would be better friends.' The mother's plea seemed to enable Visha to reveal how frightened she was, how she felt she had to hold together in case her mother might have a nervous breakdown. 'Why even my grannie, the rock of Gibraltar, is shattered.' We suggested that Visha's demonstrated strength might be at some cost to herself in terms of her having asthma. 'I am strong—I only get ill—I cannot cry.' We suggested that together we might explore her thoughts and wishes about father's death. Her reply was, 'I never thought about it—and I couldn't believe it had come true—I never thought about it as a murder story—(pause)— something had to happen I guess.' This was the end of our session and Mrs Hill handed us a poem Visha had written for us to read outside. It was about 'Jimmy' a most friendly spider who lived behind their TV set, who took very good care of himself and was no trouble at all but, the poem stated, if Jimmy were to be lost and never to return, then all the family would 'grieve' for him.

We took this poem as a directive from Visha and her mother. We felt this indicated they both were wanting to grapple with the feelings of loss and to grieve. We felt that by giving us the poem they were helping us to focus on this indeed painful area—a pain not only felt by the family but by the full team; for any loss, particularly loss by death, stirs up in all of us our own painful memories which then makes our avoidance of these areas in our work with families seem natural and understandable.

The next meeting we returned to find Visha in an asthmatic state. We took our direction from her poem and tried to link her feelings of loss and her inability to feel grief with her asthma—suggesting that the feelings seemed to be stuck inside her in an almost smothering way. Visha rejected this and was cross with us for talking such nonsense—however she was then able to reveal her horror of death and her fantasy of what it would be like to die in different ways and which would be best. Her mother helped her with this, thereby revealing some of her own concerns and fantasies.

We will follow with excerpts from a process recording, of a taped session to illustrate this mother and daughter's attempt to work together at the working through process of grieving by coming to grips with their fantasies and horror of the external reality of death.

Ninth session, third home visit

Mother began to talk about death by leukaemia and how painful that was, she encouraged Visha to share with us her solution for cancer. Visha said she thought doctors should put cancer patients to sleep. 'Cancer is horrible—death is horrible.' (She has difficulty in breathing.) Mrs Tuters focuses her back on father's death. Visha said, 'having a heart attack is like a big bursting . . . . It's like swelling up and bursting.' Visha pauses, 'which is better than being blown up and having yourself all in little parts. To die of a heart attack is better than dying of cancer, or smallpox—if you are blown to bits, like a bomb falling through the roof then that's OK because you don't know what's happening—but Daddy was in one piece.' She pauses, 'a bomb would have been better, he was in one piece like a human being.' Mother adds reflectively, 'asleep, dead asleep'— referring to the actual words Visha used when she came downstairs after finding her father. Visha continues, 'I think a heart attack is better than cancer.'

A long silence, then mother reveals her feelings—'there were things that were left unfinished—all that he wanted to do—if one could communicate with the dead one would ask him if he'd like to finish things and the obvious answer would be, yes', and with a voice hardly audible, 'why did it all end this way?'

Visha's breathing had become more troubled. Mother continues, looking at her and says, 'Daddy would have liked to carry on and was stopped—I get angry about that!'

It seems that Visha and her mother, in an attempt to grapple with the fact that father is dead, then begin to work on their relationship and the establishment of a communication and common ground between them.

Mrs Tuters asks the mother to clarify what she means by she gets angry. Visha interjects sharply, 'I don't feel angry about that.' Mother tells about all that her husband was doing. 'Maybe it would have been simpler if I had died.' Visha retorts, 'It wouldn't have been simpler—it wouldn't have been nice at all—it would have been just the same.'

We wonder aloud if Visha is saying for a little girl losing a parent, either parent, is not easy. Her breathing becomes difficult as she says, 'we both miss Daddy very much—if Mummy had died I would have missed her very much', and turning to her mother, 'if you had died I'd feel the same—if you had died you would have lost Daddy just the same—if you had died it would only be you who would have lost Daddy—you wouldn't miss anyone—I would have missed both.'

We checked out what she said, that she would miss Mummy or Daddy a great deal—that she misses Daddy a great deal—that she loves Mummy and Daddy a great deal. A silence follows.

Visha's asthma had subsided and we prepared to leave. We all walked to the door in silence. There seemed to be a mourning—a reverence was felt, all felt sad, ourselves included.

Psychological tests, two sessions

At this point Visha was seen on two occasions for testing and was given intelligence and projective tests. Her behaviour during the tests seemed in direct contrast to her behaviour in the conjoint sessions and at school. She was responsive, cheerful, talkative and dealt with the tests in a light-hearted co-operative manner.

Home visits following psychological tests

We were greeted by an excited happy Visha who was eager to talk about the tests and how much she had enjoyed doing them. Mrs Hill confirmed this, saying she had never before heard Visha laugh and be so free. On the floor close by, we noticed for the first time a doll lying in her bed. We felt the testing had made it possible for Visha to get in touch with the little girl parts of herself as she struggled with the big girl parts of herself.

Mrs Hill talked sadly about her husband and their marital problems. Visha talked about the nice times she and her father had had, she as Daddy's little girl, when they went out to concerts and films, leaving Mummy behind. Visha admitted it hurt her to leave Mummy at home and she worried about her.

Later Mrs Hill told us of Visha's love of the cinema and Visha trotted out her favourite stars. She was preoccupied with the lives of Marilyn Monroe, Judy Garland and Gene Kelly. As we listened and tried to explore and understand her world of the cinema she began to connect bits of the stars' lives with her own life. Mrs Hill said she thought Visha used the films to escape from the unhappiness in her home-life. Visha agreed and told us her favourite song was 'I'm always chasing rainbows' and then launched into a scathing attack on the unreality of her father's and mother's life—how she saw them both always trying to escape from their own reality and chase rainbows—always wishing for silver linings but never doing anything concrete about it. She moved back through her parents' relationship to where she felt a stand could have and should have been taken. She revealed her mother's abandonment of her at age five when her father brought another woman into the house. Visha blamed both parents for this and angrily told how lost she felt when she woke up one morning and her mother was gone.

The themes that emerged and were struggled with next had to do with anger and responsibility. Both Mrs Hill and Visha vividly recalled the day of father's death and mother told of her hysterical screams and attempts to bring her husband back to life. Visha told of the anger she felt towards her half-brother and sister for not being sad at the funeral. Both appeared more able to tolerate painful feelings and could be angry and sad. Mrs Hill acknowledged how she now could feel sad without feeling hysterical—saying she could face the reality of her husband's death. Visha complained of feeling ill and wanted to go to Ceylon to a new life away from the dull boring one without father. She seemed to be struggling with giving up her father and her special relationship with him. She became directly angry with her mother who was helping her understand her feelings.

We saw this anger as Visha's defence against feeling sad over father dying and her having to give up the father/husband of her dreams. We felt her anger towards her mother was at two levels—for being her father's wife and for facing the sad reality that he was dead. Mrs Hill appeared soft and sensitive and we saw her as beginning to accept herself and her sadness.

Visha next presented a change. She reported at school she was able to stand up for herself and could get mad back at the children who angered her. This change was confirmed by the school. She no longer worried about her mother at home—her worry before was that the house would burn up or her mother would run away. Visha said she liked to be treated as a person, not a thing, and we were treating her like a person by listening to what she had to say.

Around the emerging theme of responsibility, Mrs Hill dealt with her new role as a single parent and her responsibility as a mother. She expressed guilt at not having been a good enough mother in the past. We helped Visha look at her responsibility for her part in the 'shuttlecock' position. She told us two dreams—one was of all three of them in Ceylon and suddenly father dies; in the other all three and father's girlfriend were on a train, mother tells the girl off and all three live happily ever after.

Feedback of psychological test results: one session

Visha was found to be of about average intelligence with strong imagination and considerable artistic ability. The projective tests confirmed the clinical evidence that she was having difficulties in establishing a firm relationship with her mother and seemed to fear that her mother would leave her. The tests showed an air of superiority and her need to ridicule things.

These results were fed back by Mrs Waterfall to Visha and Mrs Hill. Mrs Tuters was present to help the Hills make connections between the test results and the material of their sessions. The tests gave a picture Visha had of her mother—a provider of good things, a controller and comforter, yet a mother who was worried about the impression she made—a weak childish person who fled from unpleasant things. Mrs Hill's reaction was to say she had always felt Visha wanted a stronger mother. Visha confirmed that she did but also felt maybe she would not be able to talk to her if she were. 'I like my Mum the way she is.' Mrs Hill tearfully admitted that she had never said that before.

We were aware of the reality of the strong mother who lurked in the background, maternal grandmother who was reported as waiting anxiously for the return of her prodigal daughter.

Saying goodbye, clinic visits: two sessions in one week

The final two sessions were back at the clinic. As we were unsure, the Hills made the decision, they asked if they could come back to the clinic because they felt it was their way of showing appreciation. The sessions in the home had made it possible for Mrs Hill to enter her husband's room, thus his world, a place she had never really been before. She had saved dismantling his room until the very last, until she was able to say goodbye. She now felt ready to say goodbye to us and to her husband. She reflected on the sessions in the home and how much she and Visha looked forward to our knock on the door. It made her feel good to let us in for we had heard them when we knocked. Visha reflected how nice and cosy the room was for us—how they left the heater on all night and made coffee in the morning.

Visha found it difficult to face the fact that she would no longer be seeing us. She preferred to talk about her school friends and saying goodbye to them. We attempted to bring her back to the here and now. She could not look at or speak to Dr Holland—only to Mrs Tuters. She insisted she would see us again as we would always remain in the clinic—and if we were not there then we would be somewhere. 'If Mrs Tuters were dead, if a bomb dropped on the building and killed her, then I would know how to look up her certificate of death.' As she explored this separation she managed to keep Dr Holland alive, ideal and good—as she mangled Mrs Tuters with bombs and death. She reflected on the lovely time she had with Dr Holland in the beginning, just the two of them together talking and playing. She told us she had made cards for us and was careful to point out the one for Dr Holland was the best—she liked the others, but not as much as his. She also had gifts for us but alas had forgotten to bring them. When Mrs Tuters queried the anger she might feel at having to say goodbye and at Mrs Tuters for having spoiled the lovely time she was having with Dr Holland, she readily acknowledged it. She said it would have been much better to have kept them all separate like in the beginning. Mrs Hill challenged Visha and let her know she was making her angry with the noble superior way she was talking.

In the last session Visha came in and slumped in her chair, she sprawled herself out not looking at anyone. Her posture was commented on as her being able to let go and not having to be so controlled and rigid as she was before. Visha said she was very angry at her mother for all the horrible things she said about her being noble. She felt anger at both her mother and Mrs Tuters, who she said attacked her mercilessly. She felt her only friend in the world was Dr Holland who protected her from vicious attacks. Both Dr Holland and Mrs Tuters tried to have Visha see us in terms of her own world and suggested maybe the feelings she had for Dr Holland were like her feelings for her Daddy and maybe she saw Mrs Tuters like her managing grannie. 'Not one grannie' she retorted, 'but three in one.' We all laughed together. Both Visha and Mrs Hill remarked on how similar Dr Holland and father were in appearance. This was a similarity we had been aware of ever since our first home visit, but were not comfortable with how and when to use this coincident. Mother, reality-testing, asked if we found them off-putting, for she finds friends want nothing to do with them. We talked about the problems death stirs up in others, including ourselves, as we were only human.

Visha produced her gifts. She proudly extolled their virtues and hoped we would like them. She asked if they could write and we answer. We assured them we would.

The gifts were fascinating—at the time we were deeply moved by her wanting to give us something to remember her by. They assured us they would never forget us and they hoped we would not forget them. They used the gifts as linking objects.

In retrospect the gifts seemed to spell out Visha's life as it was. To Dr Holland she gave a wooden sculpture depicting the Aesop's fable of the stork helping take a bone from the fox's mouth. She did not know the moral nor the story. We were left to surmise that it had something to do with a stronger helping a weaker. The wooden animal figures suggested to us more fantasy than a live person.

To Mrs Tuters and Mrs Waterfall she gave carefully hand-made Ceylonese dolls. Mrs Tuters' doll was a tea-picker, possibly a busy doing grannie? Mrs Waterfall's doll was a bead-seller—possibly a tempting mother/friend with things to give and sell? We were left wondering if the gifts represented Visha's life when we said goodbye, for she was off to Ceylon with a live mother, to stay with a live grandmother—leaving her dead father, the fable, the wish, the dream behind her.

Conclusion

We feel we have given evidence of growth but we do not suppose the growth has been achieved once and for all. We feel our intervention dealt with the strengths, thereby affirming the coping mechanisms of this mother and child, making it possible for them to continue to grow and develop.

One of the most important things we did was to re-establish the mother and daughter in their appropriate roles, for when we began, these roles seemed to be completely reversed. The mother was weak and dependent; she had never been mothered herself, being brought up by servants, and married a man, with previous children, who took over the mothering role of Visha. The daughter was strong and self-reliant; she had been so for a long time in her unhappy home situation, and had developed psychosomatic problems as her way of coping with her painful feelings coming from her own and her parents' unhappiness.

In terms of prevention, as referred to by J. Hutten (see chapter one) we feel we have successfully intervened in this family's cycle of pathology which justified for us the use of time and of scarce resources. In twelve weeks we had seventeen sessions, in varying combinations and locations, which we feel we used effectively. The move from clinic to home helped us deal with the fantasies and the external reality of the father's death. The move from individual to foursome helped us bring into focus and deal with the transference aspects, as most clearly evidenced in the last two sessions. The psychological tests seemed to provide both Visha and her mother with a structure, a form of containment, whereby Visha could feel safe with the expression of and get in touch with her little girl feelings. She seemed to relate to the psychologist at a sibling/peer level which enabled the mother to see a side of Visha that she felt must have been present yet she had never seen before. The mother felt relieved at the appearance of this side, as was Visha herself. This restored their confidence in themselves and in each other.

Summary

By our timed and focused intervention, we think we effected a change in the family whereby the mother could become more motherly and the daughter could become more daughterly, shifts that would be of mutual benefit to each and thus break the cycle of family pathology.

Chapter seven

Intervention in a chronic situation: an illustration of brief work with elderly parents and their youngest child

Stella M. Hall

Introduction

One of the most daunting prospects facing relatively inexperienced social workers is the inheritance of long-standing chronic cases where family members have been known to and despaired of by social work agencies for a number of years. Such families tend to have had a succession of social workers who have each passed them on to another. A kind of folk lore grows up that they are difficult to work with, cannot manage a contract and could never have the experience of becoming 'closed'. To exacerbate the situation facing their newest social worker there is often a history of crime and delinquency and the feeling that the family always 'get the better' of any professional worker or contact.

The argument of this paper is that it is possible to intervene effectively in such chronic situations, the intervention does not have to be over a long time-scale but there has to be an understanding that the authority and sanction for the work has to be returned to the family members to whom it belongs.

Referral

The case illustration is that of a family who were referred to a psychiatric clinic by a social services department. More accurately, it was Yvonne who was referred because she was in danger of being suspended from school for 'disruptive behaviour and non-attendance'. Her parents, well known to social work agencies and the education service, were not interested in her and would not co-operate. So an interview with an educational psychologist was seen by the referring social worker as providing the answer. Presumably the

60

requisite answer of why she was disruptive and unable to attend school (and, perhaps, provide a new school for her?).

At the time of referral Yvonne was 14½ years old, the youngest of thirteen children all of whom had left home except her sixteen-year-old brother Stephen. He wandered about aimlessly, looking unsuccessfully for work and resented being the subject of a care order made seven months previously for non-attendance at school. People in the neighbourhood, his parents and the current family social worker thought him 'strange' and someone who was shut away in his own world. The social worker had no statutory obligation towards Yvonne but was concerned that she, too, would need to be received into care.

From the social worker's referral letter and report to the psychiatric clinic, it seemed that Mr and Mrs Gibbs, Yvonne's parents, were elderly, her father 61 and her mother 60. They both worked full time, he as a van driver and she in a school kitchen. They had been married for twenty-six years and the only difficulties they had had, which were stated at this time, were that they had found the demands of their thirteen children and the subsequent financial strain had now made them tired of and indifferent to their two youngest.

The area team social worker had known the family for a few months and said that Yvonne, apart from being very uncommunicative, was both strong willed and rebellious and was, in fact, subscribing to the family norm of non-attendance at school in adolescence. She seemed to be the only one who had not been the subject of a care order or a fit person order. The school, at the time of the referral, were getting tired of Yvonne. They had the feeling that they had given her every chance, that she had not taken advantage of this and that she was now trying to influence her old truanting friends, who had 'reformed', to also be disruptive; in short, they wanted her out of the school. The parents, the social worker inferred, had become tired from bringing up a large family and did not have much either in the way of emotional resource or control to help Yvonne, or for that matter, Stephen. Mrs Gibbs said that she was supporting the school in their desire to get rid of Yvonne and had told the social worker, 'Don't bother with Yvonne . . . you help someone else. To help Yvonne is a waste of time.' Just after the referral letter was received, a second letter came to give a copy of the school report. This said that Yvonne's disturbed behaviour was the reason for her referral to the clinic. Her behaviour in class was disruptive to such an extent that even her own peers wanted her to be removed from them as she ruined the work which they had spent hours completing! Her attitude to teachers was rude and disobedient, her behaviour out of class was unpleasant. The teachers said that Mr and Mrs Gibbs were not interested in Yvonne's progress, only in her attendance because they knew it was compulsory. Yvonne, herself, said that she would like to go to school but was 'fed up because they (the other girls) don't want me to'.

Consultation

The clinic intake committee was uncertain whether it was the appropriate agency to help Yvonne and her parents but, as was the custom, one of the social workers from the assessment and short-term intervention workshop went to the social services department area team to discuss the case with the social workers concerned. She was horrified to discover that the eleven other children in the Gibbs family (who were now aged between 17 and 26 years) had all been before the courts on charges of taking and driving away, inflicting grievous bodily harm, being in moral danger or physically abusing their children. They had also, both boys and girls, been in approved schools, and Borstals. Two of the girls had had illegitimate children, She also discovered that Mr and Mrs Gibbs themselves were really unco-operative. They were not interested in Yvonne. Stephen was probably subnormal, educationally subnormal or schizophrenic. He was very difficult at home and bad tempered with violent changes of mood. He found it difficult to work.

The clinic social worker's depression at the impact of the information about this chronically disorganized and presumably failing family was shared with those in the area team. They agreed that the Gibbs family history and the absence of any evidence of co-operation from them had caused feelings of being overwhelmed and engulfed and so they were happy for Yvonne's educational and emotional problems to be dealt with by an outside agency. As she was the last child perhaps she could be saved from the fate of her siblings by an acknowledged psychiatric agency more satisfactorily than by a primary social work service. Implicit in this seemed to be the guilt at having failed, by identification perhaps with the previous social workers, in preventing the eleven other Gibbs children from being problems. Also, with useless parents like Mr and Mrs Gibbs, nothing really could be done because they were not able to change!

To combat the depression the Gibbses evoked, the clinic social worker suggested that, whilst it may be unlikely that much change could be effected in the situation, it might be helpful to know what Yvonne's actual educational capacity and ability was and also to give her, with her parents, the opportunity of discussing this, and their wishes and plans, with a different agency. This might do something to break up the 'log-jam' which was preventing any positive feelings being expressed or any enthusiastic work being planned.

By offering an interview with an educational psychologist and a social worker to the family, although this was along 'traditional' child guidance lines, the presenting problem of Yvonne's inability to attend school could be looked at and perhaps some observations given to the local education authority.

Meetings with family members

The clinic psychologist and social worker thought it important that as Mr and Mrs Gibbs had the responsibility for making decisions in their family they should receive a letter from the clinic inviting them to come with Yvonne to a meeting. The area team social worker would know the date and time of the meeting but would not be involved in the decision as to whether or not the appointment would be kept. The arrangements failed. The letter did not appear to arrive at the family's home and the area team social worker, becoming anxious by the pressure from Yvonne's school teachers who said they had not seen her for five months, told Yvonne and her parents about a second appointment date the clinic still were offering. (Just in case that letter was lost!) (Menzies, 1960).

Yvonne kept the appointment and saw the psychologist. Her parents said that they were too tired to make the journey . . . it was something to do with school . . . nothing to do with them and the social worker (from the area team) could do what she liked. She chose to bring Yvonne to the clinic.

The psychologist found Yvonne to be tall for her age, quite smartly dressed and attractive in a pre-Raphaelite way. She looked tired and very depressed with large, dark circles under her eyes. She spoke very little and stared in front of her, barely acknowledging the other person in the room. She did say that she was very angry with her school who had moved her into a class away from her friends. Until she was returned to their form she would stay away! The only clue to her real feelings seemed to be that when she had asked her mother to come with her for the appointment Mrs Gibbs had refused, telling Yvonne she was not interested. The psychologist reached the conclusion that there was no point in seeing Yvonne unless her parents, particularly her mother, came too and so arranged another appointment for the following week. In subsequent discussion with the clinic social worker the psychologist spoke about her concern for such a depressed and withdrawn adolescent and they decided that this was a sufficiently worrying situation to modify some of the clinic working methods and ask the area team social worker to bring Mr and Mrs Gibbs and Yvonne the next week. The risk in this usurpation of the parents' authority was one they were both willing to take. They further agreed to have a joint interview with the Gibbses and would invite the area team social worker to join them. They themselves were assured and comfortable in this way of working but the other social worker was more diffident. Her anxiety about Yvonne and the care she was receiving from her parents prompted her agreement.

Both Mr and Mrs Gibbs came with Yvonne. The clinic staff had not realized how old they were, and how young and fragile Yvonne was in comparison. She was completely mute in the interview. Mrs Gibbs spoke once to say that she had only come because she had been brought and anyway she had nothing to say. She was then mute for the rest of the hour. Mr Gibbs was volubly aggressive, demanding that the clinic put Yvonne to school—he had suffered when he was a boy and there was no reason why she should not. He had no responsibility for his daughter, 'the Education' had that, and now the clinic should see that she was punished and put back to school. The two social workers felt as though they had been silenced, but the psychologist noticed how alive Yvonne was to what her parents were doing and communicating, and how she was very anxious to keep in eye contact with 'her worker'—the psychologist. Towards the end Mr Gibbs indicated that although she was new 'his social worker' seemed to him to be interested in Yvonne. But interest was not enough, she should get her back to school. Everybody at this meeting agreed to meet again after Yvonne had had an individual meeting with the psychologist. Yvonne herself smiled at this suggestion and said, by nodding her head, that she would come.

Yvonne did not come. On the day of the larger meeting the area team social worker arrived by herself. Mr Gibbs had told her that he saw no reason why he should not bring Yvonne and his wife himself . . . he would take time off work and get things sorted out once and for all. But no one came and the clinic staff discussed with the area team social worker the joint feelings of uselessness they shared, how despairing this kind of family could make one feel and how often the feelings made a direct reflection of how the families themselves felt (Searles, 1965; Mattinson, 1975). An alternative day-care setting for Yvonne was discussed in some detail.

A quarter of an hour before the end of the time allocated to this interview, Mr Gibbs and Yvonne appeared, flushed and breathless; worn out by a journey involving three changes of buses. Mr Gibbs apologized for his wife's absence. She was packing as they were going on holiday at the weekend. 'It's our first holiday ever and we're going together. We're going to Germany, the kids have clubbed together to pay for us and Yvonne and Stephen will be all right— friends is going to take care of them.'

This interview marked the turning point in work with this family as it provided opportunity to confront and challenge Mr Gibbs with his need to force Yvonne to share with him the punitive experience of school. When he had paused for breath in his tale of this projected holiday, he started to complain that the clinic staff were useless as Yvonne had not gone back to school and there was no interview yet at the day-care centre either. He complained that Yvonne was not being punished enough. It was suggested to him that he wanted Yvonne to experience the same misery in relation to school as he had himself because of his feelings of closeness to her, which he tried to hide by his shouting, bombastic manner. He said this was not true, he had no feelings for the girl, he just wanted to live long enough to see her 'grown up and settled'.

When told that he was lying to himself and denying that he had any positive feelings for his daughter he became very angry and nearly crying with rage said that no one had ever dared to say that he was a liar in all his forty-seven years of working life. At this point it was possible to see and feel how hard it had been for those professional workers in contact with Mr Gibbs in the past to confront him with the reality of his feelings. By gently reminding him that his lying was to himself because he found his loving feelings towards Yvonne more painful to acknowledge than his angry ones, the interview changed into a reflective review in which both Mr Gibbs and Yvonne joined. He talked of both him and his wife being frightened that they might not live long enough to enjoy Yvonne as a grown-up woman and that perhaps it was better not to be too loving towards her so that she would not miss it when they died and it was not there. She said that she found it hard to be loving towards her parents and wondered whether they were too old to be concerned for her. The three workers pointed out how difficult it seemed for anyone to acknowledge strong feelings about love and concern instead of those about violence and anger. The clinic worker used this to put into context and affirm how important the area team social worker had become for the family and how it appeared that Mr and Mrs Gibbs had agreed to her suggestion of a day-care setting with a less obvious educational bias for Yvonne. Also they repeated to Mr Gibbs and Yvonne their experience in this interview of the expression of warmth and trust which they had seen passing between them and the area team social worker.

The two clinic staff told Mr Gibbs and Yvonne that they did not feel that they should help them as both father and daughter in this interview had shown that they could work with each other and with the area team social worker.

A subsequent brief meeting with the area team social worker was used to point up the issues which had arisen in the interview, and the clinic social worker offered to be available for consultation if the area team social worker wished to discuss the case, but that the decision about this would need to be made within the area team.

A further consultation

Five months later the area team social worker rang the clinic social worker and said that she had been thinking of changing the way in which she was working with the family as it was very difficult for her to manage Stephen and Yvonne and the parents in fortnightly interviews. She thought that it might be possible to find another social worker from the team for Stephen and wondered about the possibility of family interviews. The next week the clinic social worker met with the original social worker, her team leader and a new social worker, a man. From this meeting it transpired that Stephen had found and lost a job, but his father had become more understanding and there had been discussion in the family about his going to a psychiatric day centre. This was not acceptable to Stephen so he found himself another job in a warehouse. He was now less depressed and the area team social worker said that the encouragement and understanding he was receiving from his father was very impressive. The possibility of different ways of working with Stephen had been made by his blurting out to her, 'If you don't do something for me I'll have to go into a Home.' In this consultation meeting of the area team, discussion about Stephen's future and his ability for painting took place and it was agreed that perhaps it would be appropriate for the second social worker to take a major responsibility for encouraging this.

The second and last consultation meeting was held three months later. Family meetings—that is, Mr and Mrs Gibbs, Stephen and Yvonne with the two area team social workers—were being held. The focus of work was how the four could cope with being a unit of two elderly parents with the two youngest members of a large family, whether they could share across a time distance of over forty years and what kind of feelings adolescents might have towards parents who were old and might soon die.

Discussion

This short illustration of brief intervention into a chronic situation is an example of how it is possible, although difficult, for the course and focus of work in such situations to be changed. Busy social workers in area teams may not always have the opportunity for a more detached view of the ways in which such families perpetuate both their own lack of ego strength and the inability of social workers to attempt constructive, focused and time-limited work with them. With the Gibbs family there was the advantage of there being more than one worker for the two family meetings which enabled the area team social worker to acknowledge this as a possible method of work with the family subsequently. Collaborative work (Downes and Hall, 1975) with staff of another agency can help to place the problems of working with disorganized and hostile families in perspective and also to lessen the feelings of being overwhelmed and impotent which such chronic situations cause in all social workers. That it is possible not to be frightened and completely despairing and to share these experiences with other professionals can enable social workers to acknowledge and take hold of their own skills more firmly. The capacity of some clients, like the Gibbs family, to render one witless (Downes and Hall, in press) is a valid reason for working with them conjointly, and with a clearly defined focus. The family with a chronic pattern of behaviour can be enabled to take back the authority and responsibility for its actions if those working with it are prepared for the kind of discomfort and unease which was experienced in the contacts outlined in this chapter.

Chapter eight

Social work consultation to a small children's home

Joan M. Hutten

This particular children's home had a young and lively group of staff. The housefather's wife was a fieldwork social worker in the same borough and it was her senior who, learning of some of the needs felt by the group, suggested that an approach might be made to the Tavistock requesting a staff discussion group leader. This request was channelled through the department for children and parents and I expressed interest and willingness to respond.

The economics of this offer were perceived by me as follows:

1. This would be an opportunity to develop skills in consultation of a kind I had not previously done.

2. Since, as a social work teacher, I am increasingly concerned with the needs of residential workers and the techniques of collaboration between fieldworkers and residential workers, it would be very valuable to renew my acquaintance with the demands of residential work.

3. As an employee of a department with a responsibility for the provision of a proportion of the psychiatric and psychological services required in the borough, if I could prevent the referral of individual children this would be a very worthwhile investment of time. Earlier experience had made me very aware of the number of referrals we received from children's homes at times of crisis due to changes of staff.

4. These considerations had to be seen in relation to earlier collaboration between other members of the department and the residential services of the borough, which had resulted in recognition of the value of support for residential staff and a realization that the clinic could not appropriately provide all that was needed, and a subsequent decision by the residential services department to recruit and employ care practice officers to support staff in all residential

homes. At this point in time a start had been made, but the establishment was less than half filled.

Sanction to explore the possibility of responding to this request was, in the event, agreed on both sides and an appointment was made for me to meet twice at the home with the staff and the relevant care practice officer before the summer holidays.

Establishing the contract

This exploratory, contract-building phase was important. Before work can be done all parties need to look at, test and begin to trust each other. During the first meeting I made it clear, in response to expressed assumptions, that I had not done this particular kind of consultation before and that I would not want to see the individual children (in order to pronounce about them?). Implicit was a denial of magical expertise and a respect for them as colleagues. The housefather, a naturally talkative man, was successful in drawing his two male assistants into the discussion but there was a rather academic, general quality to the discussion with topics having a black/white polar opposite kind of anxiety; for example spontaneous responsiveness versus detached cleverness; the value of a historical perspective versus the handicap of prejudice due to past knowledge; authority versus permissiveness; determinism and genes versus family patterns; normal versus pathological behaviour; referral to the clinic versus children's home as therapy. There was a liberal sprinkling of sophisticated academic jargon but since I declined to pontificate and encouraged exploration of the mixed territory between the extremes, there seemed to be a growing feeling that a useful dialogue could take place.

In the second meeting there was a much freer discussion of their concern about how to deal appropriately with one of their 15-year-old girls. As a group they prided themselves on being permissive, but felt very uncertain what limits they should or could set. They felt very near in age to their adolescents and in need of a wisdom they were unsure they had. When should they take a stand on stealing, destruction, sexual pairing, drugs? Could they be respected as collaborators by the fieldworkers and parents or were they second-rate parents/social workers?

We reviewed these two meetings and a contract was made for one term of fortnightly meetings of approximately one hour, after which the situation would be reviewed by the administration. The purpose of the meetings was suggested by the group to be an opportunity to discuss things before they reached crisis point with the benefit of outside comment and validation.

First meetings

When our meetings began after the summer holiday, the staff and children had enjoyed a very successful continental holiday together and felt a common sense of achievement. The group consisted of the housefather, two male assistants, a woman assistant and a female student who had been working part time at the home for the previous eight months and was due to leave in two weeks. I arrived to find the home in an uproar because of the theft of the student's handbag which, quite correctly, had been left in the office for safety while she worked.

I learned incidentally that the housefather was leaving shortly in order to do further study, and that the children had known this for some time. I asked who the group thought would miss the housefather most and they were unanimous in naming an 11-year-old boy, the youngest of a family who have had several children in care in this home. They described the boy's visit to the housefather's parents' home for a week's holiday two weeks previously and his disappointment when he was not invited to accompany the housefather there the previous weekend when the theft had occurred. None of the remaining staff wanted to take the post of houseparent because of the limited accommodation, although they felt committed to the home and apprehensive that a new appointee might alter what they felt to be a congenial regime. When I said that, if I were reading a detective story, the facts they had told me to date would make me feel that this 11-year-old had an understandable motivation for stealing, this was seen as interesting and unexpected, but after animated discussion it was rejected as improbable because of other facets of his personality. There was an unsubstantiated wish to believe that one of the children from a nearby home, whose children had been visiting, was the culprit so that their in-group loyalty need not be disturbed. In the event the culprit never was established. There was discussion about what, if any, contact a member of staff who leaves should continue to have with a child who has been close to him. There was a confused uncertainty about this. Goodwill there certainly was but this was deprived of any constructive operation by, on the one hand, no inner conviction about the real importance of helping children to preserve their feeling of continuity by preparing and planning for how separations shall be managed and, on the other hand, by an unrealistic modesty about their own importance to the children, an undervaluing of themselves. My implied affirmation of their right to be professional and to value themselves evoked a thoughtful response. They raised their problem in knowing how to deal with the sexual experimentation of a not very bright, institutionalized 16-year-old who had been 'told on' by one of her peers whom they considered too prim. Should they offer the pill and complete licence or should they disallow the information as aroused by envy? As we talked, the possibility of repeated opportunities for their adolescents to discuss all facets of behaviour seemed to become an extension of their own freedom to explore and discuss; the affirmation of the child's own wish at some level to be responsible for herself and not to bring another candidate for care into being became a possibility when their own self-respect and capacity for responsible reflection were recognized. There was a real shift in focus for the group from a wish for detached understanding of odd behaviour towards understanding better ways to use oneself.

Because of overriding commitments I was not going to be able to meet them again for a month. I apologized for this and recognized with them that the ensuing month might well be stressful because of the imminent but uncertain date of the housefather's departure. I offered to make myself available at some other time should they 'phone me about any crisis they felt building up. With this knowledge in reserve, they in fact coped with a lot of uncertainty and upheaval without having to ask for an extra session.

A problem solved

Next time I came two assistant housefathers were drinking tea despondently in the kitchen, the wireless was turned on loud and the washing machine was in operation. The cleaner popped in and out and their special-tutor-attending teenager was knocking around. They said they had just been talking about me and wondered if I would come. They seemed to feel that since there were only two of them it might not be worth while, whether from my point of view or theirs was unclear. They turned off the wireless but poured more tea and showed no sign of moving to the room where we usually met. I suggested that we might move to our usual room and immediately they looked relieved and more confident. They told me about the uncertain staff situation: that the housefather's leaving had been postponed because of a misunderstanding about leave entitlement and that they had therefore been unable to adjust to his presence, his absence or his replacement. They were also preoccupied with the problem posed by one of their older boys who wanted to give up the apprenticeship he had started over a year earlier. He found the very long day at college once a week very unrewarding, had committed himself to buying a motorbike and a set of drums by instalments and had a friend who was employed in the same trade freelance and who earned two and a half times as much as he did. The staff were despondent; this was a boy they had thought of as one of their successes. They felt it behoved them to persuade him out of his wish

71

and could only think of exploiting his known anxieties about security to support what could otherwise only seem like specious adult reasoning. I asked what they could draw on from their own experience. To their surprise they discovered that both of them had made false starts before becoming houseparents; one had left college after a year against his parents' wishes but now had realistic plans for future training. In fact both would probably be leaving this post in about a year in order to pursue the career of their own choice. They told me, too, all that they knew about the background of the boy who wanted to give up his apprenticeship and it was at once clear that there was abundant reason why this boy was not yet ready to be anyone's success. The possibility of reviewing the situation with the youth, of valuing the person even if disapproving of the decision began to emerge, even that the wrong decision might not be the end of the world. Their own doubts about being valued by themselves or others made them tend to undervalue their charge's capacity for autonomy and learning good judgment. I related the importance of making opportunities to talk to all the children about staff changes and important decisions to their own experience with me that afternoon and they acknowledged warmly that they could use this.

On the day of my next visit I got a message that there would be no one there to meet me unless I could come later in the afternoon because they were short staffed. I 'phoned back and learnt that because the housefather had not yet been replaced and one member of staff was on leave one of the men would be holding the fort alone. I asked how things were in general, saying that I was sorry that I was not in fact free later in the afternoon. He replied that there were one or two things they had hoped to discuss. I offered to come at once for the remaining half-hour of our usual time and he accepted this appreciatively. As soon as I arrived he plunged straight into a description of an incident they were uncertain how to deal with. They thought that one of the older boys had taken down the youngest girl's knickers in his bedroom. She had later been on the point of telling them when he had playfully thrown a ball at her to indicate that she should keep quiet. This same teenage boy over-excited a ten-year-old boy who ran away from the home one day because of this, but on another occasion he evoked their sympathy when he wept and said how much he missed a boy who had left who was the only real friend he had ever had.

We talked about the difficulties of having to have parental control over boys so near to themselves in age, and the opportunities this provided for the children to identify with them in discussing growing up in general; needing permission to grow up, needing a model of respecting other people, not exploiting them, of managing the transitions from boyhood to adulthood, from old housefather to new; needing experience of the value of attention and listening as opposed to providing slick answers. For this staff member this experience seemed to result in renewed confidence that he could cope with such situations and that he could communicate his understanding to the others who shared the task. He told me that on the date my next visit was due two members of staff would be absent attending a short course and that I had better confirm the appointment before setting out.

Changes of staff

When I 'phoned I was answered by a new temporary housemother who had been appointed for eight weeks until the post of houseparent was officially filled. She was expecting my call and said that she was ready to meet me and one of the assistant housefathers would be arriving a few minutes late. When I arrived she told me a little about herself and indicated that she liked the atmosphere in this home and was gradually getting to know the children. When the assistant housefather arrived he was brought up to date about visitors and 'phone messages received. He looked distrait and said that he ought to go to the bank. In the event he did not do this, saying that they would just not have to spend anything until tomorrow. He told me about the case conference they had had about their difficult teenage youth and when I commented on the difficulty they seemed to feel about giving the children a chance to talk about their own situation he said ruefully that since the housefather had left he had found it more necessary to give orders and set limits without giving explanations. We explored the positive side of this inevitable aspect of the good parental role, but tried to get away from an all or nothing view. The staff group felt unsettled because of their doubts about getting a replacement for the housefather whom they could accept and I tried to use this to increase their empathy with the children and to link the relief they felt in talking about it with me to the priority they might give to talking with the children. They recognized the temptation to be busy about the house to avoid feeling despair about performing the primary task.

At the following meeting four members of staff were present, wanting to discuss two major incidents in which their difficult youth had figured. Both of these were dramatic enough to have triggered off panic retaliation from a less united staff and the thoughtful, reflective way in which they were recounted was very impressive. They all seemed to feel professional enough to want to understand rather than to react punitively and both incidents had in fact been handled sensitively and firmly. The group already recognized their achievement and when I shared this recognition they hurried on to tell me that their care practice officer had arranged for them to meet the warden of a voluntary hostel for girls who were over the statutory age for being in care. It was possible that some of their teenage girls might graduate to this hostel but the main purpose of the meeting was to hear about the group discussions that the warden used in order to promote self government at the hostel. They were stimulated by the prospect of this meeting and had decided that they would have a group discussion with their children too, so that they would have something to contribute. Could they please talk about the sorts of issues that might come up? We rehearsed the issues that they wanted to ventilate and there was a general air of purpose, good morale and readiness to share with the children the facts and uncertainties about staffing changes.

I suggested that they might think about reviewing our work together and we agreed that at our next meeting we would review their experience with me in readiness for the policy developing meeting between residential care staff and clinic staff that had been arranged for the end of the term.

The review

When we met the group were eager to tell me how satisfying and successful their group meeting had been; many issues had come out into the open and been honestly responded to by the total group. Staff and children had clearly experienced relief and confirmation of their individual and collective authority in handling the household's interpersonal relationships. Subsequently when the staff met the hostel warden and discussed her efforts to help her girls with the anxieties of living in bed-sitters and being responsible for themselves, they felt exhilarated that they were already making a start on helping the teenagers to think about being responsible, as was evidenced by their thoughtful participation in the group and by the fact that the boy with peeping Tom inclinations had himself now asked if curtains could be put up in the bathroom and lavatory, had started budgeting realistically and had volunteered to repair the door he had recently damaged.

No doubt the euphoria following these experiences contributed to their evaluation of my meetings with them. They expressed this emphatically as a feeling that an outsider can be dispassionate and can help them to understand why what they have done intuitively is right so that they can refer usefully to their own experience in new situations. The fortnightly interval between meetings seemed to make both continuity and autonomy possible.

The next meeting was to be our last. I arrived to find the entire staff already discussing hard. One member had been off sick with an infection and had come back still feeling very depressed about what 'the System' does to children in care and to those who care for them. The discussion ranged over idealism and realism; we/they; passivity and activity; what are reasonable goals and expectations for damaged children? How much firm framework, holding, containing and how much participation and shared responsibility is appropriate? What does professionalism imply? Perhaps it is an ability to mediate society's continuity of care without necessarily providing that care continuously by the same people: helping children to preserve their own continuity through change. Real families both nuclear and extended were felt to be irreplaceable: imitations, and poor imitations at that, are not what residential child care is about. Perhaps homes do provide peer group support for children with a limited potential for relating to parental figures?

The imminent stress of Christmas and the appointment of a new housemother, whom they had met but could only feel both hopeful and apprehensive about until she actually arrived, and their awareness that I did not know what decision would be made about whether regular consultation would be able to continue in the New Year were all being struggled with, strongly and realistically. They felt able to ask for what they knew they needed and were worthy of getting. I could only acknowledge warmly how much I had enjoyed working and learning with them.

Caring for the carers

When I reflected on this time-limited piece of work and on the themes that had come up, it seemed worthwhile to describe the sessions in some detail as illustration and evidence for the theoretical considerations that seemed to me important. The here and now of the interaction with me mirrored in a very valid way the challenges of their work with the children. 'Caring for the Carers' can sound a slick slogan if it is seen in a disenchanted, cynical we/they context. It can give a rich reward for a modest input if the identity of interest of the 'we', the professional staff of the supportive agency, with the 'we', the professional staff of the children in care, is recognized and valued.

During periods of staff change and unrest the number of children referred to psychiatric clinics escalates remarkably in our experience. If only one child had been referred for psychiatric assessment and possible placement during the period in which I was available for consultation, the input of scarce resources would quickly have exceeded that which was in fact made without anything like the same benefit to the institution as a whole. The ripple effect of high morale is inestimable and is a powerful argument in favour of putting scarce resources into initially hopeful rather than into hopeless situations. Nothing succeeds like success. If we could be omnipotent and right all wrongs, we would be just lazy if we were to give only to those who already had something. Given the reality of human limitations, my view is that in both the short and long run it is better to achieve something within a defined framework than to fail altogether. Small successes can be extended but persistent failure is demoralizing and defeating of all effort and all honesty.

An interaction that lends conviction to a model of professionalism rather than substitution or imitation carries an incentive to development. Similarly to reflect on problems and make sense of them in retrospect contributes to a store of wisdom which makes it possible then to draw on personal experience in order to understand another's situation. Affirmation of things well done reduces anxiety about coping, so that the potential skill of both children and staff can be harnessed rather than inhibited. Trust between management and external consultants can be built up only out of experience. If the primary task of the agency is clearly defined, the consultant's attention, listening and trying to share understanding hardly poses a threat. In some ways, having neither tangible resources nor power, the consultant has to rely entirely on the resources within himself. This is possibly the most potent thing there is in the field of child care and human relations.

Chapter nine

The relevance of short-term contract concepts for the training of educational psychologists

Elsie Osborne

Introduction

The educational psychologist has traditionally made extensive use of tests, especially in the areas of intelligence and attainment, and training in their administration and interpretation is still a significant component of the postgraduate courses for educational psychologists. Nevertheless their role as psychometricians has been widely questioned within the profession in recent years. This is partly linked to general loss of confidence in IQ tests and their abandonment as part of the general method of allocating children to secondary schools, but also because the psychologists themselves often felt frustrated by the marginal contribution their test results made either to the assessment of individual children in the child guidance clinics, or to appropriate and feasible educational recommendations in the school psychological service.

At the height of their popularity the claims for long-term prediction by psychological tests were, no doubt, excessive, but now there is a danger that the care in construction and standardization and the advantages of really expert administration and understanding will be undervalued.

In the cases to be discussed tests have provided the basis for discussion, on short-term contracts, with individual children and with families. Attention has always been given to the writing of comprehensible reports and the trainee educational psychologist has been expected to develop skills in communicating his assessment findings to professional colleagues. The passing on of test results to parents has been more usually confined to a single interview, part perhaps of a session with another team member, and rarely including the child. It may even still happen that a colleague is responsible for communicating the psychologist's findings; this was certainly at one time the model in most child guidance clinics.

77

Over the years the psychologists at the Tavistock Clinic have explored many different models in the belief that it is possible to communicate much more to the parents and in a way which increases their understanding of their child, and that the children themselves are entitled to much more feedback than a reassuring comment at the end of their efforts.

The single reporting back session was found often to have left families with misperceptions and misunderstandings; distortions were introduced after the session and even apparently straight-forward findings appeared to be misheard or not heard at all. Where the results were likely to raise anxiety it was found that parents could forget that they had ever been told anything, or might later claim that the comments had been entirely reassuring.

Where the family entered into long-term treatment such mis-understandings might gradually emerge and be clarified, although this was unlikely to be transmitted back to the trainee psychologist, who could be left feeling that his work had been of comparatively little significance to either his fellow team members or to the family.

In those cases in which assessment and short-term work were the basis of the contract with the family such issues as incomplete and distorted recollections became crucial. Within the department for children and parents at the Tavistock, therefore, it became much more common practice for the psychologist to spend two or three sessions with the parents or family after administering the tests.

At the same time it was found that the children themselves were interested in their results and able to accept discussion, often with relief, of areas where they found difficulty as well as an account of where they had been successful.

What test results meant to Lesley

The following is an account of a case in which the main focus was on discussion with the individual child. Lesley was a bright girl, who had been successful in her primary school in spite of a very mild degree of cerebral damage which affected her motor control. Scarcely noticeable except to the very observant, the additional strain it imposed was not apparent until she transferred to secondary school at eleven plus. There she began to disappoint her teachers and doubt was expressed about her basic ability being as high as had been supposed in the junior school. She was referred for testing and her results on the Wechsler Scale confirmed that she was much above average. She herself was told that she had done very well, that her results were within the top 2 per cent for her age group and that she therefore had good reason to expect to be quite successful in her school work. Lesley appeared to accept this explanation.

When, towards the end of the session, an attempt was made to clarify the purpose of the visits to the clinic, Lesley became rather angry, attacking the way in which she had not been told enough about the reason for her attendance, did not know why she was coming, what it was for, directing her complaints diffusely and, it seemed at the time, unreasonably. She did, however, agree to return after a full account of what it was hoped the sessions could achieve, and of the limitations, especially that the psychologist was not arbitrarily going to decide on a change of school as a consequence. On her next visit, Lesley began with another outburst, and her anger about not being told why she was coming was linked by the psychologist to the lack of adequate information about the tests she had done so far (i.e. the WISC). At this she exploded angrily saying, 'I was told I was in the top 2 per cent, it's ridiculous.' It was suggested that she work through a different test (the Progressive Matrices) but that this time she should describe the way in which she worked at the problems. She entered the task with high motivation and explained how she tried to find a solution to each matrix. She worked intelligently at each problem but gradually two specific areas of difficulty, likely to be related to her limited cerebral damage, were recognized. Lesley herself was encouraged to verbalize them. When working at some items which she found especially difficult, Lesley would make up her mind to a solution, not find it among those offered, and become fixed and unable to shift. With support, but not prompting, she could change her approach.

The second difficulty she described as being 'at looking at things as a whole'. She looked at bits and tried to solve those, yet felt this was inadequate.

This led to an acknowledgment that when this happened in class she panicked, and then acted 'stupid' in the hope of gaining attention. Thus she opened up a new range of feelings about herself, but from this the discussion returned, after a while to the basis of her problems arising from 'how I think'. She explored, calmly now, the frustrations which could arise from the high expectations which resulted from her general intelligence, contrasted with the occasions when she had difficulty with certain kinds of work which other girls found comparatively easy.

Lesley agreed to a visit being made to her school and specified which of the teachers she thought it would be best to see. She also discussed how her parents should be informed but refused an invitation to be present. She was very keen that these reports should be done soon.

After the interviews with her teachers and parents Lesley was seen again. It became apparent that she was attempting to apply her increased understanding of herself over a wider area but anger and frustration appeared once again. This time she claimed that she was not receiving enough help from the psychologist. Much of the session was spent in discussing what might be available and appropriate including her demand to see a psychiatrist because of her fears about her brain. This was agreed by the psychologist, only if further meetings made the reasons more clearly relevant, since the request was made in a way that implied the psychiatrist might have a magic solution. Lesley agreed, saying that she hoped he would hypnotize her, after which she would be completely changed.

Two further interviews were arranged, but the question of transfer to a psychiatrist was not raised again. At this point it seemed important to confirm to Lesley that she was sane, that her 'thinking' difficulties were quite different from madness, and that the psychologist was confident of her abilities. Only on this fourth visit had it become clear that anxiety about madness had been behind the initial outburst over coming to a clinic and this was made the focus for subsequent discussion.

In the last session the discussion returned to performance at school, to plans for the future, the influence of her parents' high expectations and hopes for her and to her friendships, in particular how friends made allowances for each other. This time no further arrangements for meeting were made but follow-up at school some months later revealed good progress in work and easier relationships all round.

The opportunity for the psychologist to work on a short-term focus with a family was, naturally, especially likely to arise where the problem presented was around schooling. Here the intelligence tests results were of special significance to the family, maybe the reason for referral. The likelihood of referral by the parents themselves and a high level of paternal involvement were common features. From junior age on this was something in which fathers expected to take an interest. A first interview sometimes established that the educational problem was, at a quite overt level, nothing more than a ticket of entry for other problems but in most cases, even though other difficulties might be revealed more or less openly by the family, the focus on school remained the prime issue.

In one instance where the demand from the parents was for the psychologist's support in a battle with the local authority to allocate their child to a different school, the tests were used not only to discuss the options available but to focus on the extent to which the son's own feelings were being lost sight of in the feud. In talking to him he revealed his longing for certainty and peace. Although it became clear that the boy was involved in a wider network of family uncertainties these were not taken up at the time by the psychologist but the focus kept firmly on the schooling issue, around which there was an immediate need for resolution. In spite of some angry and stressful exchanges these very caring and thoughtful parents accepted the responsibility for making a decision and apparently continued to try to sort out some of the other issues which had been indirectly raised. Some months later at their own request they returned and arrangements were made for them to work with a family therapist.

What test results meant to Charles's parents

The case of Charles was very different. Here the parents were seeking a final, definitive answer to the question of whether their son was slow at school because of brain damage or because of severe emotional disturbance. Intelligence and projective testing suggested a boy of below average intelligence, under-functioning, depressed and with a pattern of results which did not rule out some brain damage but suggested that this was not the most significant feature. Only slowly did all the previous efforts to get a certain and final diagnosis come to light, but the results of previous tests, including neurological ones, had been equally inconclusive, and had been used to emphasize one aspect or the other, so that the parents were now divided themselves. Their distress over the nature of the 'damage' their son had suffered was considerable and they sought some resolution to their feelings of responsibility and guilt as they trailed from one expert to another. In the course of four interviews shared by the psychologist with an experienced social worker the focus very gradually shifted to the feelings between the parents about responsibility and support. Charles was included in these meetings and expressed his own point of view including his feelings about his more successful younger sister. As a result, a new short-term contract was made between the parents and the social worker to help separate out their own feelings about Charles and each other, alongside efforts to seek suitable educational support for Charles. Within this time they withdrew their over-protective attitude towards Charles a little and were already able to allow him more freedom to grow up.

Frustrations and rewards for the tester

Working with families in this extended, reporting-back way, often gave a great deal of satisfaction to the trainees and was well within the scope of a year's clinical training, provided they were given regular, supportive supervision.

Sometimes when they worked alongside staff members the latter were very much aware of how the self-imposed limitations of this technique could also be frustrating. Trainees rarely had the opportunity to experience at first-hand longer-term follow-up and in many other cases it was apparent that no further intervention was likely.

These feelings were very clearly expressed by the trainee involved in the following illustration.

Georgina was the younger of two daughters in a middle-class family. Her father and sister were particularly academic and the parents had high academic expectations for Georgina also. During her last year or so at primary school she had become very unsettled at school and more difficult at home. As transfer to secondary school was imminent the parents came with the straightforward question, 'What could they reasonably expect from her?' In a preliminary session with the parents, Georgina came across as tomboyish, carefree and unlikely to be worried at the idea of the tests. In exploring how they thought Georgina might feel about coming to the clinic it was expected that they might want to describe some of their own feelings also. In fact they said that they had hesitated to accept the invitation because the situation had now improved. Where, as here, the precipitating factor in referral suggests a crisis over schooling, efforts are made to respond fairly quickly since this is often a time when families are open to new ways of looking at problems generally and of working together. However a family holiday had intervened and so there had been some delay. Georgina's school was now emerging from a crisis of its own over staff changes and the parents thought this would make a lot of difference.

They agreed that they had a very academic concept of intelligence but disagreed as to whether Georgina was bright or not. Her mother said she was sometimes described by others as brilliant but her father thought her academic potential was poor and this brightness was only superficial.

A comment from her father about the correct spelling of Georgina's name, linked with the emphasis on her tomboyishness, raised the possibility that there might have been some disappointment at a second daughter and no son in the family, but no attempt was made to discuss this. A programme of tests and reporting back was agreed and a careful description given of what might be expected in order to prepare Georgina.

The interview suggested that the moment of crisis was past, although a decision about secondary school had still to be made. The parents were not sure that they still wanted to continue and certainly were not prepared to consider possible emotional causes. Differences between the parents in regard to Georgina had been hinted at, although there was no doubt that this was generally an able and well-functioning family.

The trainee who tested Georgina was surprised to find that, although rather boyishly dressed, she was not tomboyish in manner but rather gentle and reserved as well as very tense and nervous. She tested above average on the Wechsler Scale, her full result being within the top 10 per cent of her age group; but she showed considerable lack of confidence. When asked what she thought was her best subject at school, she responded unhappily, 'I'm no good at anything.' Georgina was told about her results and openly expressed her amazement.

It was planned that in reporting back to the parents some emphasis would be placed on Georgina's lack of confidence as well as a full account of her test results, since it was felt her mother and father had little awareness of this aspect of her. Her father was especially surprised at this picture of a diffident, self-critical girl who felt that her strong points were of no value because they were not academically relevant as she understood it. That meant, apparently, that she was not good at those subjects, especially mathematics, at which her father and sister excelled. Her father wondered whether he had not been too harsh in trying to coach her himself and thus had made her more anxious. Indeed so concerned were both parents that they apparently forgot the very positive aspects of the findings. Her mother recalled battles at home and thought she had probably nagged her too much and helped to provoke the attitude of not caring which they had initially described.

A further meeting a fortnight later suggested that they had given a lot of thought to the question of future schooling and they were encouraged to discuss its suitability with the headmistress of the very academic private school for which they had originally been aiming. They were given other leads but were left to make their own subsequent enquiries about alternatives. It was agreed to meet again in six months.

At the end of these meetings the trainee commented openly, at a case conference, on her strong feelings of frustration. She felt that little had been achieved; problems had been hinted at but not followed through, and at the end there was no certainty that the family would follow any of the more promising suggestions, nor maintain their less pressing attitude. There were unfilled gaps in the account of the family's history and no invitation to make any firm recommendations or intervention.

For instance, no arrangements were made to visit her current school. It had emerged as important that the parents themselves wished to put things on a better footing by talking to the headmaster. Giving up the idea of a very competitive, ambitious school when Georgina transferred, was something they were tussling with and it seemed reasonable to leave the judgment as to how she would fit in to the possible future headmistress and themselves. A principle of this kind of advisory work is to leave the maximum possible amount of initiative, investigation and, of course, choice to the family. In this instance the parents had seemed genuinely shaken in their confidence in their own judgment and efforts were made to restore this, whilst giving as much factual information as possible.

The basis of an assessment in questions of schooling is to look for areas of match and mismatch, i.e. between child and school (e.g. academic abilities and school standards), between parents' expectations and child's performance or potential, and hopes often not previously made explicit, between the social backgrounds of home and school, and agreement or disagreement between the parents.

In this family the lack of such a match was apparent at several points. Georgina's mother had hopes, albeit obliquely expressed, that her second daughter was brilliant, which was not really so, and therefore pushed and nagged her; on the other hand her father dismissed her as non-academic and carefree, which was not true either; he undervalued her talents and it seemed likely that he nursed a private regret that she was not a boy. They both saw the primary school's fairly free approach as at odds with their rigorous ideals but had not previously looked at this as a family until the issue of secondary school made it immediate and pressing.

The trainee also felt that her testing had been limited since she had not been encouraged to do projective or personality testing which might have amplified her picture of the underlying problems, since it seemed unreasonable to raise these when it had been made so clear that no request for therapy or longer-term work was wanted by the family. Instead it was hoped that the apparent goodwill at the end of the brief series of interviews would help the family to return if problems persisted.

All the same, some gains could be specified. There was some evidence that Georgina herself had shifted in her self-evaluation and the parents had accepted the challenge to rethink their own picture of her. At first they had responded by blaming, partly themselves, partly the school and had then sought some reassurance. When reminded of her positive attributes they began to relate their new picture to other aspects which had puzzled them in the past, including the bad areas in the relationship between Georgina and her mother. Moreover many of Georgina's comments had shown how important was father's opinion to her, and keeping him very much involved was a particular aim. By coming into a deteriorating situation and working to obtain an agreed statement of the problem, it was hoped that the family would then mobilize its own resources with minimum dependence on outside help.

Among the themes not taken up were the query about Georgina's acceptability as a girl, some aspects of the bad relationship to her mother, the role of the successful older sister, and the underlying differences between the parents. There was no reasonable indication that further direct probing would contribute to the family's ability to solve the problem it had brought, but they were not ignored because they would have been uncomfortable. Subsequently, however, the psychologist felt they might usefully have looked rather more at the older sister's secure role as the 'clever one', and perhaps have involved her in the discussions.

The final frustration for the trainee was holding back from giving the parents her own opinions in favour of a more relaxed, informal kind of school.

Almost exactly six months later a friendly, detailed letter was received from the parents, followed by a telephone call from Georgina's mother asking if they still should come for a follow-up appointment. The situation was enormously improved, and Georgina had heard that she had been allocated a place at the most sought after of the state secondary schools in their area, and they had decided together with her not to continue with their request for a place in the private grammar school. They made it very clear that Georgina had been fully included in the decision and was very pleased with the school place offered. The school staff were said no longer to be expressing concern about her but above all, what emerged from the letter, was their pleasure in the improvement in the situation at home. The family had enjoyed a good Christmas holiday together. Georgina was more friendly. It seemed that her parents had made their own efforts to respond to her. Her mother summed it up, 'We don't glare at each other any more.' It was agreed to leave matters there with the offer of an open door for the future.

Preventive intervention

The case of Bruce, a 6-year-old, also illustrates the limitations and uncertainties of much brief work, but also shows how rewarding a timely intervention with a very young family can be.

When they came to the clinic in the early summer Bruce's father was just completing his professional examinations. The young wife was very much preoccupied with three small children, of whom Bruce was the eldest, the youngest being just a few months. Their letter suggested some concern about Bruce's poor progress in learning to read and a desire to pick up any problems at an early stage.

In their first interview they described their attempts to help Bruce to read at home, but he became giggly and tried to divert them into play. Ordinarily Bruce was very good at occupying himself with his toys, since his mother was so busy with the younger children and his father unable to share much in the responsibilities because of his need to study. Although his mother felt that she was left to carry most of the day-to-day responsibilities the attitude of the parents towards each other and the children showed concern and affection. In the past Bruce's father had enjoyed Bruce and played with him freely, but recently this had not been possible.

The picture presented suggested a little boy under some pressure to manage a great deal for himself at a time when his mother was herself feeling especially pressed. In order to check this supposition more objectively the parents were invited to describe his level of social competence and self-help using the Vineland Social Maturity Scale as a guide. The questions on this scale explore various areas of self-management in a fairly broadly based way, which can then be scored according to a very detailed scale of items based on an age scale.

Bruce obtained an exceptionally high score for his age. He managed his own toilet and dressing completely, was reliable and responsible in occupying himself, alone or with his friends, and helpful at home. Much of this was perfectly appropriate for a 6-year-old and the parents' responses made it clear that he had always been very forward in this respect. Whilst proud of his self-reliance, as the evidence was collected his mother commented, 'I think we don't always appreciate how mature he is.' His father added, 'Maybe we have asked too much of him.' Talking to each other, as well as to the psychologist, they remembered how, when he had wet the bed, he had become very anxious, going to the lavatory frequently during the day although they had not made any fuss but had helped him to manage for himself at night with a pot by his bed. Now they recalled that when they were talking, playing or generally paying attention to him he forgot all about it. In order to help his reading they had withheld reading stories to him unless he took his turn in reading to them. Anxiety over his dependency had been expressed in a story of a visit to stay with a nearby aunt of whom Bruce was very fond. He had stayed overnight before but on a recent visit he had developed a 'bad eye', could not sleep and eventually had asked to be fetched home. They wondered now whether he was perhaps seeking some way of obtaining more of their attention. Both parents seemed very moved by their attempts to see the situation from Bruce's point of view and appeared very thoughtful when they left.

Bruce's test results varied from good average to above average but his reading was at about a 5½-year level, where he could recognize a few words by look and say. When the tests became difficult for him he suggested, very charmingly, that he would like to play a game. In response to a lesson on letter sounds he learned with some coaxing but eventually asked to draw. In his drawing he and his mother were painting the sitting room. His patchy test results seemed a measure of the extent to which he committed himself to a task, unusually so.

The Vineland Social Maturity Scale was again used as a basis for exploring his self-management, this time from his own point of view. He contrasted his own ability to dress and bathe himself with the help which the younger children required. When asked about his drawing he said his daddy had been busy but soon his exams would be finished and then daddy would play football with him again. He grinned broadly when he added that next time he came daddy would bring him.

His parents were told that Bruce was probably potentially of above average intelligence but functioning much below that, especially in formal classroom work, using charm and stubbornness to avoid difficult tasks and investing instead a great deal in appearing responsible and grown up. Nevertheless he could be persuaded to extend himself in a learning situation and there was no evidence that he had a specific reading disability (the word dyslexia had been mentioned at one point). They responded with an account of their own thinking since the previous meeting three weeks before. They had now dropped their insistence on his reading before he could have his bedtime story and felt they should recognize his need for some babying. They wondered how they might use games to help him learn and his father began to devise some possibilities. They seemed very ready to experiment and had been trying different approaches. The relaxation of their demands that he should be independent had resulted in something of a collapse in his self-assurance, since he now refused to stay away overnight. It was agreed that this had its positive aspects since his previous independence had seemed to be at the cost of some stress to himself. However the reality was that his mother would still have to cope to a large extent on her own for some time. His father acknowledged Bruce's need for him and discussed how he might try to meet this, reassuring Bruce about the length of the absences from home which were likely to be necessary, and about his eventual return.

In response to a follow-up letter six months later his mother said that Bruce was still behind in his reading but had been getting some extra help and was now top of his group. He was willing to read to them at home and they were no longer especially worried about his progress. Bruce's attachment to his father was very clear and even though he was often too tired to play with him they would sit quietly 'almost going to sleep together'. The year had been a strain but these were particularly resourceful parents who were managing well. Since the family would soon be moving away no further follow-up was arranged.

The particular constellation of good intelligence test results, a very high score on a social maturity scale and reading retardation without other difficulties (e.g. behavioural) being apparent, is one in which children can get stuck. The opportunity to intervene at an early stage, as in Bruce's case, had preventive implications which seemed reasonably justified.

The short-term work described shares many of the principles described elsewhere in this book. Where the focus on educational issues is chosen by the families and is accepted as the framework for the contract made with them, the psychological tests are given a particular significance and the manner of their feedback is crucial. The cases described here tend to be of this kind but the lessons learned about the task of reporting back were applied by the psychologists whenever they had carried out tests.

It is now their practice to set aside some time for discussion with all but the youngest children; and the children are invited to be present when the results are given to the parents. The family's good use of time to think and come back for further discussion has been apparent in so many cases that this offer is made as a matter of routine unless there are strong reasons against it. The need for an adequate number of reporting back sessions is often clear enough when the tests have raised uncomfortable issues or when major decisions, about schooling for instance, are at stake, but what appear to be reassuring results are not always appreciated as such by the family, as when Lesley eventually revealed her disbelief in being 'in the top 2 per cent'. Far from increasing the family's dependence upon the psychologist, this more intensive approach has been found to make it more possible for families to mobilize their own resources. The direct comments about the tests have also been interpreted in a wider context as when a child's anxiety about uncertainty over exams was picked up and related to the general manner in which a family lived, often making decisions at the last moment, seldom planning outings, for instance, in advance. Although they did not, of course, change their way of life overnight, they did report more sensitivity as to where and how this might affect their son.

Sometimes increased insights into wider areas of conflict, e.g. the differing expectations of the parents, did lead a family to seek more intensive help, either short or long term, but the psychologist's intention was not to guide them specifically in such a direction. On the contrary, the expectation was that such short-term contracts would provide an economical intervention. The focus on the tests could, in these circumstances, provide a task-orientated approach which was helpful in terminating.

Chapter ten

Brief focal work with Israeli families under stress

Eva Sternberg

Introduction

Stress has been apparent in the lives of the majority of the Israeli population over the last three decades. The last war, October 1973, with its many tragedies, brought about an urgent reappraisal of the methods available in the country for coping effectively with a population at risk. Mental health workers were requested to work actively with those directly affected by the crisis. This resulted in an increased awareness of the need to implement preventive mental health measures. Inter-disciplinary team work became an accepted way of coping with urgent problems. Active group work with soldiers, bereaved parents and families showed the effectiveness of this method. Group supervision of voluntary workers made it possible to extend the work in order to meet the overwhelming need of a population in grief.

Literature dealing with crisis theory and its preventive intervention is by now well known and only brief allusion will be made here to the main concept. Caplan's (1961) theory deals with crisis as an upset in a steady state. He refers to normal critical transition periods in people's lives which require them to make new adjustments in order to meet a new situation. Drawing on the work of Erikson (1965), he looks at the transition of an adolescent into young adulthood, the arrival of the first baby, the loss of a job, a death in the family. He points out that the way an individual copes with the demands of the new role he assumes will have an impact on his subsequent mental health. The programme set up to help people early in the critical period was aimed at enhancing their coping capacity with the hope of preventing emotional disorder.

Papers reporting community studies relating to bereavement and loss have contributed to our understanding of our present crisis. Parkes's studies which he reports in his book *Bereavement* (1972a) indicate that the reaction to the loss of a loved person resembles reactions to other types of loss. I shall refer to this aspect later in the paper when describing reactions of families to a missing member. Parkes (1972b) also reports studies made on reactions to loss of a limb and loss of a home.

Perhaps one of the crucial differences in our techniques of preventive intervention as compared with studies elsewhere is the concept of the workers' own involvement. Mental health workers are usually not involved in the crisis themselves, and thus are free to assess their interventions with their clients. This allows for the implementation of a goal-orientated process to take effect within a given time limit. However, most of us were experiencing our own crisis. Thus we could not but help identify with and become more involved with our clients' distress. Most of us had either husband, son or another close family member serving at the front. Often we had had no news for weeks and the consequent anxiety was intense. We therefore set up supportive groups for ourselves where we discussed our own feelings and our reactions to the families with whom we came into contact. We examined our own state of crisis, which enabled us to continue working within the community. I remember our mutual response when as a group we were confronted by an outside expert who had come especially to offer his services in our crisis. He advised us to be more objective and directive in our interventions. Later he understood the enormous price we all paid working under stress. Perhaps our expertise enabled us to judge when to become actively involved. Often we would share silently the family's pain and we would listen and try to understand their anger. We found that volunteer workers had to be helped 'to listen' and to share without 'small talk' which covered up their own real helplessness in an intolerable situation.

Although it is still too early to assess the results of our work with families in stress, it is apparent that the large majority have been helped to utilize their own coping mechanism and have been enabled to return to their former level of functioning. The techniques used varied and I shall now attempt to describe my own experience with some of the families referred to me. I shall present four families who were informed that one of their members was 'missing'.

War and the missing

As in all wars, when the news is broadcast that hostilities have started, the general reaction by the population is one of utter shock. This initial reaction may perhaps be likened to Bowlby's (1960) and Bowlby and Parkes's (1970) theory of grief as a phasic process. The transition from one phase to another is seldom distinct and features from one phase of grief often persist into the next. Thus, the first day of the war gave rise to a feeling of numbness and disbelief like the description given by widows after hearing the news of their husband's death (Parkes 1970). The second phase brings about protest and yearning. Protest is in this case a feeling of bitterness and anger that war could not have been avoided and yearning is an intense wish to return to the former state of security and peace. The third phase sets in some time later and results in apathy and aimlessness with a disinclination to look to the future or to see any purpose in life. Anxiety is experienced and the accompanying fear has a further paralysing effect on the families with soldiers away.

When the first news of casualties came through, the reaction was an acute one and anxiety was heightened. We have noted an unusual awareness to all sounds, whether to a knock at the door, or to the ring of the telephone. It was during this unbearable state of tension as experienced by most of the population, that we as mental health workers (mostly social workers and psychologists) were asked to participate in a programme to help inform families of those soldiers who were posted missing. It had been decided not to use volunteers, who were mainly non-professional, as it was felt that a longer contact would be required for these families. Volunteers might not be able to cope with the complex reactions of these families. We decided to visit these families in pairs in order to share the burden. The families had been informed officially a day or two previously and our visits aimed at supporting the family during the waiting period until further news could be received. It was recognized that whatever the outcome, preventive intervention in its broadest meaning would be required.

We had decided previously to introduce ourselves as representatives of the Ministry of Defence (which officially we were) and not as professionals from a mental health clinic. Later, most families enquired about our professional identity and when we told them, they were mostly relieved that they could discuss some of their complex emotional problems with us. They also felt freer to bring out their anger against the authorities. Our introduction was usually made by explaining that we were concerned about the family's distress in coping with the news they had received and that we would try to ease their burden in any way possible. The family's reactions to our visits, and their own reactions to the news, varied greatly and depended on their previous coping capacity, their ethnic background and other factors which I shall elaborate later.

The H family

The information given to us was a mere slip of paper on which was written a name; that of the missing person and his next of kin, with address. Thus we came to the door of a family living in a new block of flats. A tall, dignified man with a long black beard and dressed in the clothes of a Hassid[1] opened the door. He introduced himself as the brother to Mrs H. The room was full of family and neighbours who dispersed into other rooms when we arrived and when they heard who we were. Only Mrs H, her parents, brother and children— a girl aged 4 years and a boy aged 6 years, were left. The family was a deeply religious one and the women wore a sheitl[2] and scarves over their heads. The men were dressed formally. The family was dignified and controlled. Mrs H looked pale and red-eyed. She was in her fifth month of pregnancy. The children whimpered and ran about aimlessly. The old parents sat quietly in a corner. It was Mrs H's brother who started to ask pertinent questions. What information had we? Did we know more than they had been officially told? They looked at us blankly when we responded negatively—hardly comprehending that we could come and sit there and not come up with some positive information. We sensed their unverbalized anger. That first visit we listened to them describing the man who was missing. He had been the sole survivor of a family killed in the holocaust. They recalled the details about his last day at home, his work, his interests and his love for his children. Above all the family's main concern was that he would be found alive and be returned to them. We shared their pain without saying much. We asked whether we could return and see Mrs H on her own a couple of days later? She welcomed the suggestion.

The second visit was made while the children were at school. Mrs H was not on her own. There were neighbours and her parents present. We asked to talk to her alone. She sat down with us and began to talk about her fears. She started to cry and told us that her gynaecologist had informed her that there was some doubt whether the foetus was alive. She had had previous difficult pregnancies. Her parents had to return to their home far away and she was without a telephone. She needed help with shopping and with the care of the children. The latter were becoming difficult, refusing to eat properly and sleeping badly. She herself said that she felt irritable and had lost her appetite. As a result of this visit we arranged for the installation of a telephone which to our surprise was completed within a few days after a visit by us to the main communications office. The usual waiting period for a telephone in Israel is approximately three years. We organized a volunteer (with Mrs H's consent) to help her with the shopping and with the care of the children in the afternoons. (We had previously applied to WIZO[3] for a volunteer and had interviewed her personally to ascertain if she could be of real support.)

Our visits continued approximately weekly and we began to know the children and neighbours. The family had moved to the area only a few weeks previously from another town. Mrs H's pregnancy was progressing all right and she was telling us that actually she could now cope somehow. She felt that she did not like being at the receiving end for during the Six Day War she had been a volunteer herself helping families with their grief. She was never left alone and had the support of constant friends and relatives around her.

As it came nearer to the date of the publication of the list of prisoners held in Egypt, Mrs H became extremely irritable and her former state of despair returned. She could not sleep, she wandered about aimlessly and the children again became difficult. We visited her more frequently again. Families were informed personally the day before the official publication of the list. She waited, no one called. Her husband's name was not on the published list. In desperation she took her children, left home and travelled to her parents' home three hours' away by bus. On arriving there she was contacted urgently by the Ministry of Defence and was informed that her husband had after all been one of those returned home. He had been injured and was in hospital.

The family gathered together and rejoiced. They held a special ceremony to celebrate the rebirth of their lost one. Our contact ended and we followed up the family's health by telephone and were told that Mr H had recovered and was returning to work. They thanked us, but we were not invited to join them in their special celebrations.

The family's coping capacity enabled them to continue functioning during the actual crisis. Their strong religious beliefs with the family's close-knit relationship supported them and gave them strength to continue. Palgi (1973) describes the reactions to mourning and bereavement among different ethnic groups and poses the question whether these variants have been sufficiently understood in the light of these groups' social and cultural resources which are of utmost importance in any programme of rehabilitation. The H family's resources no doubt made our brief intervention effective. Mrs H needed our external support which we provided quickly and efficiently. She dismissed us as soon as the crisis ended and with this we had completed our goal which was to enable this family to continue to function as normally as is possible in a stress situation.

The L family

The address to which we were directed was the home of the young wife of the missing soldier. There was no answer to our knock, but a concerned neighbour gave us the address of her parents. On being met by Mrs L's parents we realized that we would be involved with three families: i.e. Mrs L, her parents and the husband's parents. All were in a state of crisis. Mrs L's mother was tearful and depressed; her father was quiet, subdued and wandered about aimlessly. They told us that Mrs L was newly married and was in her sixth month of pregnancy. She was spending the evening with her parents-in-law. We then continued on to the husband's home, where we found neighbours, friends and family assembled together with Mrs L senior. After the preliminary introductions, we were bombarded with angry questions. They accused the authorities of failure. They were angry with the officials who had imparted the information. They were angry with us for coming with empty hands, that is, merely coming to listen and to offer useless help, and not bringing any real information. They more or less told us that they did not need our help, as they could manage perfectly well on their own.

Mrs L sat numbly, a little removed from the family and hardly said a word. Towards the end of this first meeting we asked to see her on her own, to which she vaguely agreed.

The L family was a closely knit one, not religious, and the young couple were both Israeli born. They had met in the Army. Both had a younger brother also serving in the Army. Their parents were of Polish origin and were of a good socio-economic level. Mr L's parents were young, in their forties, and Mrs L's parents were older and less active.

On this first visit to the home of both parents, we listened and said little. We were shocked at their pain and at their anger. We too felt numbed and returned home in pain. We wondered what we could do to help these families? We realized that the H family had not had this impact on us on our first visit. They had appeared dignified and more in control of their feelings. We wondered whether the Hs' religious values helped them through their crisis. This led us to evaluate our expectations of our contact with these families. What right had we to intrude into the very depths of a family's private world? Could they in turn expect anything from us? Could they make use of our specialized knowledge? As our contact with the L family continued we could finally answer this question in the affirmative.

This family did their utmost to trace their missing member. They applied to the foreign press, to the local press and to the United Nations Organization. Mrs L senior became a member of the Parents' Committee for the missing. They made personal contacts with soldiers who had been together with their son at the beginning of the war. They were convinced that they had identified him on photos which were open to inspection to the public. Photos taken by the foreign press of prisoners held captive in Syria. Mrs L junior remained composed and lived on in her world, somehow removed and detached. She refused to discuss her pregnancy. For her the pregnancy was terminated at the sixth month. She finally condescended to attend a class for preparation for childbirth, a month before the date of delivery. In the meantime, she dutifully visited her parents-in-law daily and spent the day at her parents' home. She had left her own flat.

Our regular visits continued to the two homes. Often we found all the shutters down in Mrs L senior's home. For weeks she shut herself in and refused to go out. She would get up only in the evening when her husband came home from work. Sometimes we found her ready to talk to us alone. Her guilt at mourning her son was overwhelming. She verbalized her distress that she was reacting to her son's disappearance as though he were dead. She tried to hold on to the hope that he was alive, but the effort was enormous. She lost weight, had sleepless nights and became listless (Parkes and Brown 1972). She tried to pull herself together for her daughter-in-law's sake.

The two fathers were more active, showed less overt emotional behaviour. They showed no sign of tears and attempted to control their feelings. Yet, they were unable to sit down for any length of time and would aimlessly wander up and down the room and would make themselves busy with tasks formerly allocated to their wives.

The family finally pulled itself together with the imminent arrival of the baby. Mrs L senior started to leave the house and shop for the baby. She opened the shutters of her house. We made arrangements with the physiotherapist and with the local hospital's maternity department to give special care to Mrs L junior. The physiotherapist agreed to be on call in order to be present at the birth. Mrs L junior still refused to discuss the birth of her baby and automatically did what she was told without affect. But we would often find her red-eyed and depressed on our visits.

The birth was uneventful and Mrs L junior requested only minimal medication. She wanted to be fully awake at the crucial moment. The physiotherapist encouraged her and for the first time Mrs L started to talk about her husband. She told her baby girl that her father would be proud to have such a beautiful daughter. The family was relieved that the baby had arrived normally. They shared their feelings with us when we visited the hospital. They busied themselves with the newcomer and the baby became the focal point of their activities. Mrs L junior was now more open to discuss her husband, but always maintaining that he was alive and that he would return to her and to his daughter.

As with the H family, when the news was announced that a list would be published with names of prisoners held in Syria, the family again became more tense. Their fate would soon be decided. The evening of waiting ended with the enormous relief that Mr L junior was indeed a prisoner and was alive. The family became alive and their rejoicing was boundless. Neighbours, friends, people who had kept a distance because of this family's dilemma joined them and cried with relief.

The ensuing long waiting period for the final return was hard. Mrs L junior talked about her fears of finding a different man from the one she had known previously. She became more restless and went for long walks with her daughter, pushing the pram for hours. The final return of prisoners from Syria was an event that the nation and the world shared with enormous relief. Those who were reunited were alive and life could be lived again. Those families whose missing member did not return and who watched the nation rejoice, became more despondent and their pain became intolerable. They asked themselves if they were now allowed to mourn? And would they finally find relief not knowing the last resting place of their beloved? These questions will be referred to later. The L family invited us to the special party they held in honour of Mr L junior's safe return. Our contact was then terminated with the suggestion that if Mr and Mrs L junior needed us at any time in the future we would be ready to see them. Mrs L senior offered her services as a volunteer in helping bereaved families and we arranged the appropriate contact for her.

Our contact with the L family was an experience that tested our personal and professional integrity with each visit. We often asked ourselves whether we had a right to intervene in these people's lives? And yet, we continued, knowing that we had to be consistent even though their anger was often directed at us. We showed them that we could contain and share their pain because we cared, not just because we were representatives of the Ministry of Defence, nor because of our professional status, but because we were human beings like them, and they learnt to accept us and were able to express their feelings more openly.

The S family

Mr and Mrs S have three children. The eldest was on reserve duty, the second, a daughter, is married and lives abroad, and the youngest, a 20-year-old son, unmarried, was posted missing. He was serving his regular three year national service and was an officer, respected and successful. He was planning to go to university after demobilization and had already been accepted. Mr and Mrs S were pioneers in their young days. They are of Russian origin and had invested a great deal in their children's education. The family was a closely knit one with many relatives and friends.

As with our former contacts, we found that the S family was surrounded with friends and neighbours. They were never left alone. They were able to accept us far more readily and encouraged our visits using these more purposefully and meaningfully. Mrs S returned to work and Mr S who was semi-retired, made himself busy. It was he who would serve tea, but he seldom sat down on our visits and showed his restlessness. Mrs S cried and grieved for her son. She wanted to know the exact details of what had happened to her son and was able to gain some information from a wounded soldier who had been in the same tank. The parents gradually understood that there was little hope for their son's return.

Mrs S described her feelings and her guilt at being alive. She told us one day:

'I feel the fresh air I am breathing. I feel the beauty of the sun and the beauty of the day and yet I ask myself how is it that I can allow myself to enjoy just being alive when my son is most likely dead.'

On hearing that a father had taken his life when he heard of his son's death, the couple became shocked. They expressed the need to search for a purpose in life in order to go on living.

Mrs S's sleep continued to be disturbed. She constantly thought she heard the door open and expected her son to enter. We encouraged her to visit her family doctor whom she refused to consult for weeks. She finally was helped by her doctor who then became more active in checking her health.

Our contact with the Ministry of Defence enabled us to find out more exact information concerning the son's movements during the first days of the war. We recommended that the brother of the missing soldier should be released from his reserve duty in order to be with his parents. This was implemented and he was able to support his parents in their distress. He himself became more active in searching for information.

Our visits continued and we felt deeply moved by this family's courage. They started to accept us as friends and often we found ourselves answering their questions about ourselves. They enquired about our families and our work; Mrs S showed a particular interest in the mental health services. We attempted to share their pain when prisoners were returned and when they sat at home feeling empty and forlorn. They became more distressed with the attempts made to return the bodies of soldiers from the Egyptian lines. Their son's had not been found.

While I am writing this paper we were informed, on contacting the family, that their son's body had finally been identified among the last thirty-nine bodies returned by the Egyptians a few weeks ago. Mrs S sounded very distressed and she welcomed the suggestion of our visiting within the next few days. During this last visit to the family they talked about their son coming home at last. Again they retraced the last twenty-one months of waiting and felt that time had been meaningless to them. When we said that we would accompany them on the day of the funeral, Mrs S commented and said: 'As you have accompanied us through this period, now you'll be able to accompany our son to his last resting place.'

Little need be said about this family's courage and integrity. The extent of their suffering through this long period of waiting cannot be measured. Their legal mourning for their missing son was finally made possible by the body being identified 1¾ years after his disappearance.

The C family

The C family has not heard to this day whether their 19-year-old son's body will ever be returned to its final resting place. They have come to accept that he is dead. This family's pain was particularly intense as Mrs C had lost her husband, her son's father, a year previously. He had died of a heart attack and she had married again only recently. Mrs C's numbness and shock were so intense that her denial that her first-born was missing was complete and prevented her own family from coming to her help. Her present husband reacted by bringing out his anger with both the higher authorities and with the local authorities. The family isolated themselves from their community and their beautiful, luxurious house was usually empty and still.

I was able to see Mrs C on her own for a period of several weeks and she talked at length about her first husband and her children's reaction to his death. She went into great detail concerning his actual death and her own immediate reaction to this. We discussed her two younger children's need to express their feelings concerning yet another loss. The oldest boy had been a father to them. They both reacted to the news by becoming incapacitated. The younger boy returned to stammering from which he had suffered after his father's death. The older one reverted to severe asthmatic attacks which kept him in bed. His mother was incapable of nursing him and asked her housekeeper to look after his needs. Both boys had received therapy in the past. Mrs C discussed her second marriage to a divorcé whose two boys were also staying in the house. She felt incapable of meeting all their needs and had to be given time to find herself again.

My visits continued and I would meet the whole family, that is: the four boys and Mrs C's husband. Sometimes I joined the children in their games, or I would sit watching TV with them. Mrs C gradually started to leave the house. She went shopping and went to the beauty parlour. She drove to the library and exchanged books. She had agreed to re-establish contact with the boys' former therapist. She had framed a photo of her missing son and placed it in the sitting room where it could be seen by all.

The family indicated that they could now cope on their own and contact was gradually terminated with a possibility offered that they could renew the contact whenever they felt the need.

Discussion

The four families presented here are only a few of those who were experiencing extreme stress as a result of the war. The country is a small one and when one soldier is reported missing or killed, the nation reacts as though one of its own family members had been affected. We were all deeply involved and the consequent crisis was nationwide. I shall now examine first, the families' reactions to the crisis and their reaction to our visits. Second, I shall attempt to define our own particular involvement and the techniques we applied to each individual family.

The families' reactions

The normal loss of a close relative brings about the shock reaction which was mentioned earlier. Referring to Bowlby's and Parkes's theory of a grief as a phasic process, the Jewish tradition of sitting Shiva[4] gives formal recognition to this process of mourning and thus allows the bereaved family to express its feelings openly. The reactions may vary according to ethnic background of the individual families. When the loss is not definable, the process of mourning becomes stunted and a return to a previous, healthy level of functioning is likely to become impaired. The effect of receiving the news that a soldier is missing immediately gives rise to doubts of his being found alive. The very fact that this doubt is experienced results in an attempt to deny the event. The family desperately holds on to the hope that the missing one will return and thus strains its resources to the utmost in attempting to cope with its normal functions. The question of coping capacity then becomes merely hypothetical.

How can we then define the concept of missing in this context? The answer may be that the missing one is neither dead nor alive, but is lost. Parkes (1972b) in his paper on the reactions to loss of a limb, spouse or home indicates that loss results first, in an urge to recover those parts of the world which have been lost and second, an urge to protect the damaged self that remains. Thus, our families searched for their missing one. This took the form of heightened activity in attempting to gain detailed information up till the disappearance of the missing person. The information gained was often unacceptable or denied because it might destroy the hope that still existed. Often a parent sensed that the lost one (as experienced in actual grief) was present and had returned, especially at night when imagined noises would be heard. Referring to Parkes's concept of the individual's need to protect the damaged self, the families reacted as though the world appeared to stand still and they protected themselves by shutting themselves in and not leaving their homes.

The guilt which families experienced when their reactions became similar to those mourning their dead, further enhanced their state of stress. The usual Shiva when the mourning family is not left on its own and relatives and friends sit with the bereaved, turned into an endless, timeless 'shiva' for the majority of the distressed families. They were not left alone. It may be questioned whether some families might not have preferred to have had more privacy with the possibility to let go on their own.

How then did these families react over the many months of waiting? Mostly, the sleep pattern was affected. Loss of appetite, restlessness and irritability were experienced. Initially, anger with the authorities was openly expressed as they were blamed for the failure and consequent loss.

Individual members of the family reacted differently to the news. Fathers were not able to express their feelings as openly as their partners. Mothers cried and eventually talked about their feelings. Fathers had to be helped to talk. Their own unbearable pain that a son might in fact die before them affected their potency and enhanced their helplessness. They felt weak and were threatened by losing their authoritative role. Often they adopted tasks previously belonging to their wives. Some compensated by becoming active in committees formed to trace the missing. Children's reactions to a missing brother, father or relative were in many aspects similar to those of the adults. De Shalit (1970) writes about the children's involvement in times of war. Children are not kept in the dark for they are part of this small community and thus sense the tension. They are often called to take on responsibilities and tasks left vacant by a member at the front. In our experience their reactions indicated their need to deny the painful news and therefore they adopted earlier modes of behaviour.

The families' reactions to our visits varied. Their expectations initially were that we could provide them with the answers that officials from the Ministry of Defence had not imparted. They often became angry and disappointed when we pointed out that we were not messengers but people who could fulfil a different, but less definable role. Some were overtly angry. Others were more controlled. Later we were accepted as two people who cared about what happened to them and we became friends of the family. Sometimes we were used as go-betweens, i.e. between the families and the Ministry of Defence. Many of the families were at first too angry to visit the Ministry and therefore used us to act for them. Later, when a centre for the missing was set up with special interviewers, some of the families were able to apply directly to the centre. Sometimes our professional know-how was asked for.

Our involvement and interventions

As mentioned previously our involvement was very different from the usual contact of mental health professionals in crisis intervention work. We had to be constantly aware of our own reactions to the family's distress. This would relate directly to Hutten's (p. 41) assertions concerning the ability of the worker to establish continuity in her work through constant reappraisal of her own life experience. Our preventive work could only be meaningful through a continuing contact with the families. The length of the contact varied, but initially our visits were frequent and intensive. The focus was mainly on the here and now of the stress reactions. Sometimes past experience had to be worked through as with the C family concerning earlier uncompleted mourning. When further urgent problems arose, such as the arrival of a baby (the L family) we increased our visits. In fact, with each additional stress (e.g. publication of prisoner lists, the searching for bodies) we needed to react in a flexible way (Pincus 1974). We learned to cope with our own pain by discussing our feelings after each visit and participating in groups with other professionals doing similar work. We became aware of our own coping mechanisms and thus were able to set boundaries for ourselves.

Often we experienced a sense of failure, for the family's despair could not be lightened. We had to accept our own limitations and respect the families' different ways of expressing their pain. The L family often tested our endurance as did the C family. Our contacts with outside agencies, e.g. WIZO, the communications centre, a hospital and the Ministry of Defence enabled us to help solve some of the urgent practical problems which the families themselves were as yet incapable of solving.

Perhaps the contact with the H and L families gave us some indication that our visits had helped these families in bridging a very stressful period. They were able to revert back to their former state and continued to function as normal families. The S and C families are still experiencing stress and as yet have not been able to return to their former levels of functioning. It is too early to evaluate whether our visits helped in allowing them to express their feelings more openly, thus enabling them to gain understanding of their own, rightful reactions to death and grief.

Summary

Four families who were confronted with the news that one of their members was posted missing are presented. The families' reactions to the news was discussed. The concept of the term 'missing' is examined in the light of the Jewish and ethnic framework of the individual family. The hope that the missing person would return prevented the families from indulging in the normal grief reactions. Guilt was noted when family members succumbed to expressions of mourning. The expectations of families and workers was often found to be diametrically opposed one to the other. The workers' own involvement had to be constantly reappraised in order that the contact could continue to be a meaningful one. The focus was directed towards helping the family throughout the stress period. Two families were enabled to return to their former levels of functioning. The other two are still undergoing stress. One has now brought home the missing member and can mourn officially, but the other is still not able to mourn meaningfully.

In our experience the concept of brief focal work with families in stress is particularly relevant during a national crisis, when a preventative mental health service is confronted by a population at risk.

Notes

1 Hassid is a very orthodox Jewish religious sect.
2 Sheitl is a wig worn by married Jewish orthodox women.
3 WIZO is the Women's International Zionist Organization.
4 Shiva is the official seven days of mourning.

Chapter eleven

Short-term contracts in general medical practice

Mannie Sher

The project

This chapter on short-term contracts in general medical practice is based upon the work of the community unit of the adult department of the Tavistock Clinic (Brook and Temperley 1976). The work of the unit involved a number of Tavistock Clinic workers of different disciplines, each trained in psychotherapy, being attached to a medical group practice in the north London area for one session per week over a period of two or three years. The aims of the attachment were to study the contributions made to general practice by the presence in the surgery of a psychodynamically-trained professional person.

In Great Britain, the local general practice down the road is for many people the place to which they can turn not only for their medical complaints, but also for help with their psychological and relationship problems. It has been estimated that between 40 per cent and 65 per cent of ordinary referrals to the local doctor may mask an underlying problem which the patient is unable to articulate, but for which he is seeking relief. Many GPs feel ill-equipped to address themselves to personal and family disturbance that often lies behind the symptom of the sick patient. The introduction of the psychodynamically-trained worker into general medical practice is an attempt to reach various crucial groups of people in stress before their difficulties develop into chronic problems requiring the deployment of major psychiatric and social work resources.

The presence of dynamically-trained workers in the surgery is not only limited to helping patients in trouble e.g. married couples, young parents, those with problems associated with loss—separation, sickness or death—but it is also an attempt to provide a supportive network to the practice staff members. In a paper by Brook (1974)

103

he states that 'in any situation of responsibility people are faced with a dilemma. This is, how to carry out the work, and how simultaneously to cope with the anxieties that arise from it.' In our time-limited attachment we found it was often more profitable and economic to provide not only a direct service to patients, but also to create opportunities for the surgery staff to discuss and attempt to understand the feelings generated in themselves by the patients. This, we found often resulted in the making of more appropriate decisions with and on behalf of patients.

The practice

The four surgeries in the project, each with a Tavistock worker attached, are situated in the north and north-west area of London. The practice to which this writer was attached was rather like a health centre, with a large patient population (17,500) and a large staff (6 GP partners, 3 assistant GPs, 2 liaising health visitors and 12 nursing, reception and administrative staff). It had extensive links with existing social, psychiatric and other medical services and this fact helped us to explore and understand the complexities of liaison, referral, and multiple care of patients. For example, it was not uncommon for case conferences to take place in the practice involving the presence of local authority social workers, educational psychologists, mental hospital psychiatrists, school teachers etc., thus underlining the philosophy of whole-person medicine with the local general practice serving as a central base for patient care and decision-making (Graham and Sher 1976).

During the session in the surgery the attached worker would normally see one new referral and one or two old ones for about an hour each and devote the rest of the time to discussing the outcome and future planning together with the referring GP. These meetings with the GP had a number of important functions.

(a) They underlined the importance of sharing the care of the patient. The GP retained ultimate medical responsibility for the patient but he was helped to understand some of the psychological and emotional pressures being felt and communicated by the patient. In this way the attached worker acted as a resource person to the practice for emotional and mental disorder. He acted as a frequently available 'second opinion'.

(b) By discussing the reason for the referral with the GP and subsequently seeing the patient, the attached worker was in a unique position to offer comments on what he thought was happening in the doctor-patient relationship. This often resulted in the GP feeling freer to continue seeing the patient himself in order to help with certain relationship and emotional difficulties.

(c) Following discussions between the GP and social worker the result may have been to offer the patient further limited sessions with the social worker in order to concentrate on one or two areas of difficulty in the patient's life. The patient would be offered a time-limited contract of between three and six sessions in order to help him face some of the emotional problems that might underlie his symptoms, thus providing a little relief, and also reassuring the patient that it was safe and acceptable to share personal difficulties in the setting of general practice. It may have been decided to leave matters open, with the patient free to return to the social worker, and certainly to the GP, at any time the patient felt it necessary to do so; or the decision may have been taken to refer the patient (patients in the case of marital couples and families) for specialist help. When this happened the contract between patient and worker had an element of extended preparation for formal referral and psycho-therapy. This was beneficial in the case of anxious patients who required gentle preparation over time on the familiar and less threatening territory of their local general practice.

Some theoretical considerations

A review of the literature reveals an optimism in the use of short-term contracts in the fields of psychotherapy and social casework. Hutten, in the first chapter of this book, asks whether there are any magical short cuts in social work interventions or whether there is a real theoretical backing for planned short-term work. A brief, but wide-ranging review of the literature by Hutten reveals almost unanimous support in favour of brief contracts and intermediate goals. Tuters, in discussing brief focal intervention in family mourning, points to the benefit and value of limited (seventeen sessions) and goal-directed work to a family in crisis to help affirm its strengths and coping mechanisms making it possible for them to continue to grow and develop.

Balint (1973), on the other hand, in discussing research in psychotherapy suggests that in the brief contact between doctor and patient (usually between five and ten minutes) one is not concerned to find short cuts to the longer psychotherapeutic interviews. Instead he encourages the development of a new technique, able to be practised within the average time available, which will help the GP understand the patients' conflicts, followed by the use of this understanding with therapeutic affect. Salzberger-Wittenberg (in press), too, in discussing brief counselling and psychotherapeutic consultations with young people, refers to the wisdom of having only simple and reasonable goals in brief work. These are: to help the patient to *find out* something about himself and his problems; to *think and feel* about them, and to *take stock* of himself. She warns too, that brief intervention should not be seen as a kind of speeded-up psychotherapeutic process, which might have the same results as long-term treatment. Neither should it be seen as a panacea to solve the scarcity of or unavailability of psychotherapy resources. For the therapist it should not be regarded as a substitute for on-going intensive work with individuals which sustains the hard-won sensitivity and openness to unconscious processes. Short-term work, in other words, depends upon long-term training, if the worker is to be enabled quickly to discern, grasp and articulate the crucial features of the patient's emotional life and his transaction with the worker.

Malan (1963) gives attention to the development of this new technique and the skill in practising the technique. One of the characteristics of successful brief psychotherapy, he suggests, depends as much on very stringent selection criteria as with the technique itself. The conditions of successful focal therapy according to Malan are:

1 The patient's willingness and ability to explore feelings.
2 The patient's ability to work within a therapeutic relationship based on interpretation.
3 The therapist's ability to feel that he understands the patient's problem in dynamic terms.
4 The therapist's ability to formulate some kind of circumscribed therapeutic plan.

To this list can be added another condition: Malan demonstrated that working in a group, with a common purpose and enthusiasm had a considerable influence on the results of his research. Thus high morale and group support were important in maintaining a level of enthusiasm for this type of work.

It emerges then that short-term work, while obviously effective in many instances, can contribute to a muddled optimism which leads to a belief that life-long problems will be cleared up, that it can be practised with any patient in any setting. Almost all writers point to the importance of selecting patients who will respond reasonably well to a short-term intervention. These will be patients whose level of disturbance is not too great, those with relatively intact personalities but suffering as a result of a crisis situation, e.g. bereavement or some other loss in which quite primitive feelings have been evoked and relived in the present. Balint cautions us not to believe that what happens in general practice can be understood purely in terms of psychopathology or psychodynamics. Instead one is observing a therapeutic process, an interplay between GP and patient, a 'space between' in which the therapy takes place. According to Balint the preconditions of the focal approach are:

1 That it is possible to isolate in the patient's mind a fairly well-defined area of the problem, e.g. an older adolescent girl, suffering from nausea and inability to separate from her parents and leave home.

2 We could possibly help the patient with that area, e.g. help her to see the possible aggressive attitude towards the parents in her continued dependency on them.

3 That readjustment could lead to important improvements in other areas of the patient's life, e.g. by finding separate accommodation and a job relationships with her parents might mature and she might find her social life more satisfactory.

The essence of short-term work would appear to be based on an ability to get hold of and understand the *simple predominant emotions* operating in the interchange between patient and doctor, patient and social worker. Brief intervention, like all forms of psychotherapy, implies listening not only to the content of the patient's statements (i.e. being illness- or problem-orientated) but being responsive to the patient's style of operating, e.g. being aware in the patient of, say, a tendency to secretiveness, denial of the real problem, needing to blame other members of the family, or the doctor, dependency, wishing to impress etc. (i.e. dynamically orientated).

Examples of short-term contract work

In this section I would like to describe some examples of work which illustrate the necessity for spending time on reflection about the patient's problem and his relationship with the GP. In the setting of general practice the oft-heard cry is 'too much work and not enough time in which to do it'. The pressure of work can often be used to avoid certain painful issues not only in the patient's life, but also in the patient-doctor relationship; issues that are avoided by keeping the patient at a distance, by offering a prescription, or embarking upon a course of action before the problem is fully understood, or by referral to the 'expert'. Frequently such quick action does not help the patient, nor does it provide satisfaction for the doctor in his work.

To understand the patient's communications better, to reach a clearer diagnosis, and to offer the patient help that would produce beneficial change, we all agreed would require time—time to think and time to plan. The following is a description of three cases where some direct patient contact with the social worker took place. In addition, important work occurred between the GP and Social Worker, illustrating the importance, amongst other things, of adequate thinking and preparation needed in making an appropriate referral. Failure to think and plan ahead carried its own dangers, as will be seen.

Case no. 1

The first case, too, is an illustration of what is achievable in a brief intervention and what is not. The patient, a single woman of 30, was helped in an immediate crisis involving panic attacks that prevented her from spending time with her family. The longer-term problem of difficulty in maintaining ongoing relationships with men required intensive individual psychotherapy which was not available in the general practice and may not have been acceptable to her there, anyway. The patient, Miss C, had had a fairly consistent contact with her GP, a man much older than herself, a fact which later turned out to be significant. She longed to have a close relationship with a man, but scornfully rejected all her partners. Available men were treated as babies, not worth very much if they showed any interest in her, while unavailable and married men were viewed with distant fascination and admiration. She was utterly contemptuous and denigrating of women, particularly those who worked under her, whom she viewed as potential rivals, needing to keep a careful eye over them, since she believed they coveted her position as head of a large department. Her suave and chic exterior, giving the impression of 'being on the town every night' belied a sad, lonely and frightened little girl who stayed indoors, fearful that others might discover the truth about her.

She revealed that her father, who had died ten years before, had been strict and puritanical in his attitude towards her, but a lot more relaxed and easy-going with her sister, two years younger. Miss C, although her father's favourite, felt extremely hostile towards him for being so restrictive, and immensely rivalrous with her sister, who was allowed to smoke and date boys at a much earlier age. The patient's mother was quiet and reserved, suppressed by her husband, suffering quietly under his domination. Six weeks before the father died the patient quarrelled with him and they were not speaking to each other at the time of his death. A few months later the sister contracted Hodgkins disease from which she recovered, but was left unable to bear children. Miss C expressed strong angry feelings towards doctors for misdiagnosing her sister, but this, she hastened to add, did not extend towards her GP, whom she felt cared for her in a way her father had not.

The GP had independently referred Miss C to a clinic for psychotherapy, which she attended for one appointment only. She experienced the referral to the clinic as an abrupt ending to a developing warm relationship with the GP. No sooner was she able to express positive feelings towards the GP, through the mist of anger and mistrust towards the medical profession, when he referred her to someone else. She felt hurt and rejected, another example for her of a brief and limited contact with a man. Some weeks later, after further discussions between the patient and GP, Miss C agreed to talk to the social worker, in the surgery, since this meant she was being offered further help on familiar territory, and since her contact with the GP would be maintained indirectly via the social worker. The patient was offered three sessions in all with the social worker at weekly intervals, which she first accepted, but later resented because it was yet another example of a 'three-week affair' with a married man that offered no hope of fulfilment.

In the preparatory discussion between the GP and social worker reasons for the referral were adumbrated. These were: (a) to extend the assessment of the problem, (b) to ascertain whether limited help, through reflecting and thinking about her problem, could be offered in the surgery, and (c) to work through some of the patient's hostile feelings that would become manifest at the end of the contact.

Between the second and third sessions, over the Easter vacation, the patient was expecting to return to her family in the country, and since she experienced feelings of panic when she was with her family, it was thought that help in this area would provide a useful short-term focus. Consequently during the first two sessions the material centred around, first her fear of expressing loving feelings towards her father, which also meant she could not show grief when he died, and second, her intense but denied feelings of rivalry towards both her mother and sister. Competition in sexual terms was seen by the patient as punishable by death. Her sister, the main sexual rival, becomes stricken, and her mother, also a rival, is denigrated and relegated to an insignificant, servile position. The patient can therefore not allow herself to be successful with men, because to be so means first eliminating, and in unconscious terms killing off, her rivals, something she feels she has already accomplished in relation to her mother and sister. To expiate the guilt that is aroused, the patient enters into impossible relationships in which she is bound to be rejected and hurt.

The result of these discussions was the expression of sadness and shedding of tears for the first time in ten years which afforded the patient much relief. After recovering, and with great mirth, she said she could not accept such emotions in herself.

Later, during her return home, she was amazed to discover that she was able to discuss her feelings of jealousy so openly and honestly with her sister and mother. They both said they had known all along of the patient's jealousy towards them and were surprised that she remained unaware of her feelings. The family went out together over the weekend and the patient experienced none of the panic feelings she had come to expect in their company.

Miss C returned for the final session astonished that her symptoms had cleared up so dramatically, but remained sceptical over the permanency of the 'cure'. She felt she needed longer-term therapy and was dismayed that she could not continue with the social worker. She wanted to know where else he worked and became increasingly angry at a system in which one had to be either very ill or very rich to get treatment. She raged at the recurring pattern in her life of intense but brief contacts with men, at the end of which she felt rejected and humiliated. Her disappointment and frustration were recognized by the surgery team and having been articulated by the patient herself, she felt freer to accept referral to a clinic for longer-term psychotherapy.

Discussion

This example illustrates how easily the caregivers can ignore the warm and affectionate feelings the patient is trying to communicate to her GP because the style of communicating is defensively off-hand and peremptory. It also points to the necessity for recognizing the pain and sense of rejection that can be experienced by the patient in a referral. In the three sessions with the patient, she was given the opportunity to think about her difficulties with men, which extended to the GP and the social worker himself, in addition to considering her rivalrous feelings towards her mother and sister. This produced a gain in the short term, and crystallized for the patient the already half-formed idea of acquiring for herself a longer-standing therapeutic relationship elsewhere, even if this meant facing disappointment by her GP with whom she had developed close ties. For the surgery team too it was a lesson on how one can unwittingly be cast into a rejecting role even when referral appears to be, at first glance, in the patient's interest.

Case no. 2

This case of brief intervention—seeing a 45-year-old female patient, for four sessions—included the GP who was present for the first and last sessions. Most of the referrals to the social worker from the GPs were of patients presenting emotional or relationship difficulties, and in the 21 to 35 year age-group. The patient in this case, however, represented a departure from our usual practice, first on account of her age, and second because the problem was essentially a physical one with secondary, but nevertheless profound, emotional factors, interfering with the management of her treatment. The presence of the GP in two of the sessions was also different from our usual way of working and was part of our attempt to find new ways of integrating the social worker's understanding with the on-going medical care of the patient. The patient, Mrs L, suffered from chronic nephritis and renal failure. Because of her personality instability she was having difficulty in maintaining the necessary arduous dialysis regime and the hospital felt she was far too disturbed and unreliable for them to contemplate doing a kidney transplant.

We felt the patient perceived our collaboration as a respect for and insistence upon the indivisibility of her physical and emotional difficulties. She was reassured by this since she was a past-master at manipulating the surgery staff, playing one partner off against the other, playing the practice off against the hospital, and so on. Because of our collaboration she was unable to do this with us. The implications of her illness could no longer be avoided: she had the full medical facts from the doctor and could receive help with the emotional aspects from the social worker. The GP briefed the social worker in Mrs L's presence, discussing fully the medical and emotional aspects of her illness and the resulting limitations it placed on her life. No pressure was placed upon Mrs L to decide on dialysis or transplantation. The objective was to demonstrate to Mrs L that the surgery team knew about and understood her position and, as harrowing as it was, their own anxieties about the extremity of her position did not prevent them from openly facing the patient with the knowledge (privately shared by all three of them) that she was likely to die. Mrs L was tremendously relieved at this demonstration of unison and, like a child with a new gift, asked the GP if he would let her see the social worker and himself again. The task would be difficult, she thought, because she was not one to accept help easily. People trying to help her were seen as weak and needing to be fought off. Dependency made her aware of her weaknesses and vulnerability. The struggle for survival was all-important—a lesson she had learned from her hated mother, an extremely beautiful and ambitious woman, who lacked feeling altogether, determined only to climb over everyone else to get ahead. The patient's mother saw the outside world as bad and cruel, and prevented her daughter from having friends and leaving the house for more than a few minutes, until she was 16, by which time the patient was already leading a secret promiscuous life. The cruellest turn came later when the patient's mother suffered a slow, and lingering cancer, from which she later died much to everyone's relief. Would the world be pleased too when the patient herself died, she asked. She felt caught in a vice—on the one hand a fear that the outside world (her husband and children) hated her and wanted her to go, and on the other hand, an awareness of the reality that her inside world was poisoned and was slowly ebbing the life away from her.

The four sessions centred around her struggle about her physical weakness, and her bitterness that life carries on elsewhere. She expressed feelings of disappointment and anger that her weak body prevented her from enjoying things the way others did. She also came to see how, through feelings of guilt at having disobeyed, hated and rivalled her mother, she was now ensuring the failure of her treatment, by refusing to take her medication and also deliberately destroying examples of her creativity—actually setting out to destroy relationships with her children, messing her paintings and pulling out her tapestries. These actions were not only the expression of her anger and frustration, they were also a defence, she discovered, against giving up the secret thought that she was someone special, the prima donna, whose productions had to be perfect. She came to see that maintaining this image of herself prevented her enjoying the things she could reasonably expect to achieve or produce.

In the fourth and last session she turned to the GP and said that the four sessions had forced her to give up some of her dreams and the need to be regarded as special. She had been able to come out of herself and do some satisfying work. With tears in her eyes, she told the GP and social worker how grateful she was for having the opportunity to discuss the reality of her illness and weakness honestly, something she could not do with members of the family, whom she suspected of wanting to be rid of her anyway. She was able to see now that her children were important, that they genuinely cared about her, and that she could look to them to make a contribution to her life. After these sessions the patient vigorously renewed her contact with the hospital, who were amazed to see the changes in their patient. A few months later Mrs L underwent a successful transplant operation, to receive a kidney donated by a member of her family.

Discussion

Joint interviews with colleagues, as described in this case, have many pitfalls and were usually practised when the members of a team had first got to know one another well and understood and respected each other's skills and knowledge. Meeting beforehand and planning each session, preparing the ground to be covered and the roles to be adopted was important, if we were to avoid two people simply doing the same job or the patient continuing to play one member of the team off against the other. This unusually dramatic intervention, however, illustrates the enormous transformations which are sometimes possible when the unspeakable underlying anxiety (i.e. death) can be faced. Neither the GP nor the social worker on his own would have had the courage to face the patient with what she was doing to her slim chances of survival.

The GP and social worker did find themselves polarized occasionally, e.g. when the GP became alarmed at the way the social worker was confronting the patient over issues of separation and death. When it occurred we understood it to mean that unwittingly we were caught up in a process through which the patient was attempting to keep separate certain bits of knowledge about herself, knowledge that may have been too painful to consider and accept. Focusing on the limited number of sessions (four) provided opportunities to reflect upon the limitations of the illness, and to think about the realistic contributions the patient could herself make, in addition to what she could reasonably expect to receive from her doctors and family.

Case no. 3

The patient was a 21-year-old Brazilian girl who had visited a young woman trainee GP in the practice a number of times with abdominal pain. The GP had, among other investigations, given her a vaginal examination and the girl haltingly confided to her that she was very unhappy because of sexual conflicts which made it impossible for her to have a relationship with a man. The story that then emerged was that she was an illegitimate child whose mother died giving birth to her. After some six months her father's wife took her and brought her up with her own legitimate children. She felt unloved and was very aware that physically she resembled her own mother. Both her father and stepmother, she felt, made it clear that they were afraid she would behave in a sexually irregular way, as her mother had done. As a result she reacted with frigidity and terror when young men made sexual overtures to her. She fled from her family, entering this country to work without the proper papers and registering with the surgery with a false address. She had thus got herself doubly in her present life into a replica of her original position as an illegitimate entrant.

The GP was hopeful that now that the patient had told her what the 'real trouble' was she could be helped with it, but she didn't know quite how and turned to the social worker. The latter agreed to see the patient and was struck immediately by the way the patient saw her as the stepmother to whom the young GP (whom the girl quite explicitly compared with her ideas of her long lost mother) was going to abandon her. It was decided that the GP would continue to be the main professional seeing the girl, with the social worker acting mostly as consultant to the GP, but seeing the girl from time to time. The social worker felt that as well as having sexual conflicts,

113

the patient was also a very maternally deprived girl whom the GP might be able to help by offering her a little of the motherly concern and permission to be sexual which she had missed.

Perhaps just because she felt more securely understood, the patient then became markedly more clamorous, demanding a great deal of the GPs time and getting herself into hospital for the removal of her appendix. While in hospital she made a half-hearted attempt to slash her wrists and when she returned to stay with relatives she spent her time in bed, wept a great deal and refused to go to work any more.

The surgery staff and the social worker became aware that in the case of this girl the staff were driven to adopt one of two opposing stances. If they showed their concern for her they soon found themselves exploited and indulging her beyond their better judgment. The alternative attitude was punitive and rejecting. The young GP tended to get herself wearisomely exploited by the girl who rang her at home and presented her with a multitude of physical complaints which the GP strongly suspected were of a hysterical nature. The hospital staff and the senior partner in the surgery, also a woman, tended to adopt harsher attitudes. The senior partner pointed out that this demanding patient had got herself into the surgery illegitimately and she suggested she be requested to move to another practice. The social worker pointed out to the surgery staff how the patient had got them to enact on the one hand the indulgent (but punished) mother she had never had and on the other the rejecting stepmother. By keeping this phenomenon very firmly in mind, both doctors were able to check their responses and to help the patient neither regress into a manipulative collapse nor get herself expelled from the country. They were able to be firmly supportive towards her, recognizing with her how needy and angry she was but energetically encouraging her to return to work and to get her external problems (visas etc.) sorted out. The girl though still quite demanding, did make valiant efforts to manage her life in such a way that she could remain lawfully in this country.

The young GP, as a trainee, was working in the surgery for only a year. The social worker stressed to her that this patient would be very upset by her leaving and urged her to discuss it with her well in advance. The GP found herself postponing this discussion, partly from anxiety about the girl's reaction. Eventually in fact, the social worker told the girl who was upset and angry and tore up the prescription the doctor had just given her. She did not, however, make any of the dramatic self-destructive moves that the staff had feared and on a subsequent occasion asked the social worker to tell the doctor that although she felt she was often a burden to the doctor, she deeply appreciated what she had done for her and would like permission to be able to write to her occasionally in the future. It was arranged, in a way that did not feel punitive to the girl, that when the young GP left, the girl should be transferred to the list of a woman doctor in her own neighbourhood.

Discussion

The aim of the social worker's intervention in this case was to offer the patient and the GP a circumscribed contact that would help them both consider the patient's self-destructive behaviour patterns, and point to ways in which the practice team could respond to limit these tendencies, rather than reinforce them by adopting rejecting stances. There were few major therapeutic objectives. This girl's personality difficulties were profound and might well not have been amenable to long-term psychotherapy even if her life situation made such therapy a possibility. The surgery staff, with consultation from the social worker, were however able to give the girl an opportunity to experience a little of the sort of relationship she had always wanted and to help her check her tendency to wreck that opportunity. She gained some hope which may make her more able to avail herself usefully of what her new GP and other people in her life offer her.

The surgery staff learnt something of the power patients can exert to impel those caring for them to re-enact certain central configurations in their past lives; they also learnt that by spotting these processes, it is possible to refuse to accept the roles in which they are cast and by this refusal to help the patient glimpse that life need not be the way he has felt it must be.

Conclusions

The common feature in all these cases is that their contact with the social work member of the practice team, although different in character in each case, was brief. The patients were part of the ordinary general practice population, they felt free to discuss with their doctors problems of a psychological nature, and expected to receive some help or relief by so doing. Neither the doctors nor the social worker encouraged dependency in their patients; instead they provided limited opportunities to explore certain relevant areas in the patient's life and helped mobilize their inner resources and sense of responsibility for getting on.

In the first example, the patient in three sessions received immediate help involving anxiety attacks, and was helped to decide on more formal psychotherapy for the longer-standing difficulties of her relationships with men. She was helped to reach this stage of thinking, through the warm contact and sense of trust she developed with the GP.

In the second case the problem was primarily medical, but in four sessions, two of which were joint interviews, involving the GP and social worker, the patient was helped to stem her self-destructive trend and view her treatment and relationships with her family in a different light. In effect, this intervention may have saved her life.

In the final example, the primary consumers of the social worker's services were the surgery staff themselves, who were helped to see that their inter-professional relationships were being invaded and dominated by dynamics arising from the patient's personality difficulties. By discussing these relationships with the social worker the surgery staff were able to disengage themselves from reactions which were primarily a function of the patient's inner world.

These three brief examples give an idea of the variety of problems that present themselves in general medical practice and which may be amenable to short-term intervention by a dynamically-trained social worker. The way the patients presented their problems was different in each case and so was the outcome of the intervention. There were no pre-arranged goals, and the aims were carefully discussed between the GPs and the social worker on each occasion.

Short-term contracts in general medical practice may be the appropriate form of intervention for a number of reasons. First, social work attachments to general practice are usually short—three to four hours a week, and it would be uneconomical to fill the time with a few long-term patients.

Second, general medical practice, by definition, is open-ended. Patients come when necessary and stay away if they feel like it. Brevity of contact, and use of short-term interventions is often a function of the patients' reluctance to continue in a more intense therapeutic relationship. They may not wish to involve their doctors with deep personal problems, preferring to keep these problems either private or else dealt with in another place by an unknown person.

Thus, we found the more successful referrals were those where, in the mind of the GP and the patient, the reason for the referral was further assessment. This raised no false hopes and there were no commitments. There may have been therapeutic spin-offs during the assessment phase, enabling the patient to manage more effectively, but essentially the purpose of the referral in the first instance was, together with the patient, to understand his problem a little better. Patients for short-term intervention within the setting of general practice were rigorously selected—those requiring longer-term psychotherapy were helped to find their way to a specialist clinic or agency if they were so motivated. In such instances, the social worker with his knowledge of available facilities acted as a resource person in the practice.

Brief therapeutic interventions, extending to half a dozen sessions, took place with selected patients, where it seemed clear that by paying attention to the simple (but often very disturbing) predominant emotions, following a discernible, recent crisis, maximum effect could be gained with minimum expenditure of time.

It cannot be sufficiently stressed that the chances of effective brief intervention depend on one's ability to understand and grasp the central dynamic issue facing the patient and the doctor.

Conclusion

The work that has been described has all been done in or emanated from a psychiatric teaching clinic, yet, in much the same way that the short-term contract philosophy has been rewardingly applied in the training of other disciplines (of which Elsie Osborne's contribution is one example), so a great deal of what is learnt in one setting can be applied in another. All social workers have to manage themselves; work in all kinds of agencies can be enhanced by 'stopping and thinking' instead of rushing into precipitate action. The discipline of finding the minimum that needs to be done by the worker so that the client can have the achievement of doing the rest for himself can be applied in any setting. Techniques are only appropriate if they are appropriate. Values, attitudes and skills can address themselves in an infinite permutation of ways to changing challenges and resources. Values have largely remained constant, though with different emphases, throughout the history of social work and the task of making a personal and contemporary synthesis of available knowledge in relation to values and attitudes is the business of each of us individually and collectively.

Further reading

An article by P. Argles and M. Mackenzie (1970) in *J. Child Psychiatry*, 11, pp. 187-95, Pergamon Press, Oxford on 'Crisis intervention with a multi-problem family—a case-study' includes a useful discussion and 22 references.

Juliet Berry (1976), *Daily Experience in Residential Life*, Routledge & Kegan Paul, further discusses the crucial importance of caring for the carers.

Douglas McGregor (1960), mentioned in chapter one because of his open theory of creative management which is as applicable to social work agency organization and client contracts as to industrial processes, stimulated his students to explore the applications of his theory X and theory Y. Readers who would like to follow suit might read Edgar Schein, *Organisational Psychology* (1965), Prentice Hall and *Process Consultation, its Role in Organizational Development* (1969), Addison Wesley, Reading, Massachusetts.

The most seminal book about the principles underlying the management of change and the management of loss, in whatever situation they occur, is Peter Marris's book (1974). The understanding it affords of a multiplicity of circumstances offers a very useful conceptual structure.

W. Reid and L. Epstein (1972), *Task-centered Casework* is an important addition to the references which was not available at the time that chapter one was written.

Helen Perlman, writing in the *Clinical Social Work Journal*, vol. 2, no. 3, 1974 about the 'Confessions, concerns and commitments of an ex-clinical social worker' makes her personal synthesis for the 1970s in a way that echoes my own in many respects.

Isca Salzberger-Wittenberg's (1970) concise and lucid contribution to the present series, *Psychoanalytic Insight and Relationships: a Kleinian Approach*, Routledge & Kegan Paul, addresses itself to many of the issues broached in this book and offers an extensive bibliography.

In relation to the whole notion of management of self, the references recommended in connection with the Tavistock 'Leicester' conferences on group relations and the experience of membership of such a conference have been particularly enriching. A contribution by Pierre Turquet on 'Threats to identity in the large group' in L. Kreeger's (ed.) (1970), *The Large Group: therapy and dynamics,* Constable, conveys vividly the anxieties connected with guarding and crossing the boundary of self.

Bibliography

Balint, M. (1973), 'Research in psychotherapy', chapter 2 in E. Balint and J. Norrel (eds), *Six Minutes for the Patient*, Tavistock Publications, London.

Barker, M. (1970), 'Education for social work: a teacher's viewpoint', *Social Work Today*, 1, no. 9, pp. 18-23.

Bellak, L. and Bellak, S. S. (1971), *Children's Apperception Test*, CPS, New York.

Berry, Juliet (1976), *Daily Experience in Residential Life*, Routledge & Kegan Paul, London.

Bowlby, J. (1960), 'Grief and mourning in infancy and early childhood', *Psychoanalytic Study of the Child*, 15, pp. 9-52.

Bowlby, J. (1969), *Attachment and Loss, Volume I Attachment*, Hogarth Press, London.

Bowlby, J. (1973), *Attachment and Loss, Volume II Separation, Anxiety and Anger*, Hogarth Press, London.

Bowlby, J. and Parkes, C. M. (1970) 'Separation and loss within the family', in E. J. Anthony and C. Koupernik (eds), *The Child and His Family*, International Yearbook for Child Psychiatry and Allied Disciplines, vol. 1, J. Wiley, New York. pp. 197-216.

Brook, A. (July 1974), 'Supporting the caregivers in the community', unpublished paper read at the annual meeting of the Royal College of Psychiatrists as part of symposium of 'Psychodynamic skills in the field of mental health'.

Brook, A. and Temperley, J. (1976), 'The contribution of a psychotherapist to general practice', *Journal of Royal College of General Practitioners*, 26, pp. 85-94.

Caplan, Gerald (1961), *An Approach to Community Mental Health*, Tavistock Publications, London.

de Shalit, N. (1970) 'Children in war', in A. Jarus, J. Marcus, J. Oren and Ch. Rapaport (eds), *Children and Families in Israel*, Gordon & Breach Science Publishers, London, pp. 151-82.

Doll, E. A. (1953), *The Measurement of Social Competence; A Manual for the Vineland Social Maturity Scale*, Minneapolis Educational Test Bureau.

Downes, C. E. and Hall, S. M. (1975), 'An experience in collaboration', *Social Work Today*, 6, no. 9.

Downes, C. E. and Hall, S. M., 'Consultation within Social Work', *Social Work Today*, in press.

Erikson, E. (1965), *Childhood and Society*, Penguin, Harmondsworth.

Forrester, R. (1967), 'The untreatable patient', *Canadian Psychiatric Assoc. J.*, 13, 3, pp. 88-290.

Geismar, L. (1969), *Preventive Intervention in Social Work*, Scarecrow Press, Metuchen, New Jersey.

Glasser, A. and Zimmermann, I. L. (1967), *Clinical Interpretation of the WISC*, Grune & Stratton, New York.

Goldberg, E. M. (1970), *Helping the Aged*, Allen & Unwin, London.

120

Graham, H. and Sher, M. (1976), 'Social work and general medical practice: Personal accounts of a three year attachment', *Journal of the Royal College of General Practitioners*, 26, pp. 95-105. Also in *British Journal of Social Work*, 6, 2.

Grygier, T., Chesley, J. and Tuters, E. (1969), 'Parental deprivation'. A study of delinquent children', *Brit. J. Criminology*, 9, pp. 209-253.

Haworth, M. R. (1949), *The CAT: Facts and Fantasy*, Grune & Stratton, New York.

Hoxter, Shirley, (1974), Contribution to a discussion re an educational psychotherapy case, Tavistock Clinic, on 4 December.

Hutten, J. (1972), 'Psychodynamic approach to casework', *Social Work Today*, 2, no. 22, pp. 5-10.

Isaacs, S. (1948), 'The nature and function of phantasy', *Int. J. Psychoanal.*, 29, no. 2, pp. 73-97.

Kellmer-Pringle, M. (1966), *Social Learning and its Measurement*, Longman, London.

Leared, J. (1974), 'The Camden bereavement project', *Midwife and Health Visitor*, 10, pp. 15-16.

Leonard, Peter (1971), 'The challenge of primary prevention', *Social Work Today*, 2, no. 5, pp. 2-4.

Lewis, Oscar (1962), *The Children of Sanchez*, Secker & Warburg, London.

Lewis, Oscar (1968), *La Vida*, Panther, St Albans.

McGregor, Douglas (1960), *The Human Side of Enterprise*, McGraw-Hill, New York.

Mahler, M. (1971), 'A study of the separation—individuation process', *Psychoanalytic Study of the Child*, 26, pp. 403-24.

Malan, David (1963), *Brief Psychotherapy*, Mind & Medicine Monographs, Tavistock Publications, London.

Marris, Peter (1974), *Loss and Change*, Routledge & Kegan Paul, London.

Mattinson, J. (1975), *The Reflection Process in Casework Supervision*, Institute of Marital Studies, London.

Menzies, I. E. P. (1960), 'A case study of the functioning of social systems as a defense against anxiety', *Human Relations*, 13, no. 2.

Meyer, J. and Timms, N. (1970), *The Client Speaks*, Routledge & Kegan Paul, London.

Miller, E. J. and Gwynne, G. V. (1972), *A Life Apart*, Tavistock Publications, London.

Palgi, Phyllis (1973), 'Death, mourning and bereavement in Israel arising out of the war situation', *Israel Annals of Psychiatry & Related Disciplines*, 11, no. 3, Academic Press, Jerusalem.

Parkes, C. M. (1970), ' "Seeking" and "finding" a lost object: evidence from recent studies of the reaction to bereavement', *Social Science & Medicine*, 4, pp. 187-201.

Parkes, C. M. (1972a), *Bereavement: Studies of Grief in Adult Life*, Tavistock Publications, London.

Parkes, C. M. (1972b), 'Components of the reaction to loss of a limb, spouse or home', *Journal of Psychosomatic Research*, 16, pp. 343-9.

Parkes, C. M., Benjamin, B. and Fitzgerald, R. G. (1969), 'Broken heart: a statistical study of increased mortality among widowers', *British Medical Journal*, 1, pp. 740-3.

Parkes, C. M. and Brown, R. J. (1972), 'Health after bereavement: a controlled study of young Boston widows and widowers', *Psychosomatic Medicine*, 34, pp. 449-61.

Pincus, Lily (1974), *Death and the Family: The Importance of Mourning*, Pantheon Books, New York, pp. 112-29.

Raven, J. C. (1951), *Guide to Using the Progressive Matrices*, H. K. Lewis, London.

Reid, W. J. and Shyne, A. W. (1969), *Brief and Extended Casework*, Columbia University Press, New York.

Robertson, J. and Robertson, Joyce (1967-69), Film series: *Young Children in brief separation;* 1967, no. 1 'Kate, 2 years, 5 months: in foster-care for 27 days', 16 mm. b & w, sound, 33 mins.; (1968), no. 2 'Jane, 17 months: in foster-care for 10 days', 16 mm. b & w, sound, 37 mins.; 1969, no. 3 'John, 17 months: 9 days in residential nursery', 16 mm. b & w, sound, 45 mins. Tavistock Institute of Human Relations, London.

Rogers, Carl (1951), *Client-centered Therapy*, The Riverside Press, Cambridge, Mass.

Bibliography

Salzberger-Wittenberg, I. (in press), 'Psychotherapeutic consultations with young people', chapter in Dilys Daws (ed.), *Psychotherapy with Children and Young People*, Wildwood Publications.

Searles, H. F. (1955), 'The informational value of the supervisor's emotional experience' in *Collected Papers on Schizophrenia and related subjects*, Hogarth Press and Institute of Psychoanalysis (1965).

Silove, J. (1976), unpublished research, preliminary findings, Tavistock Clinic, London.

Silverman, P. R. (1966), 'Services for the widowed during the period of bereavement', *Social Work Practice*, Columbia University Press, New York.

Tyhurst, J. S. (1957), 'The role of transitional states, including disasters, in mental illness', in *Symposium on Preventive and Social Psychiatry*, Walter Reed Medical Center, Washington D.C.

Vickers, G. (1972), *Freedom in a Rocking Boat*, Penguin, Harmondsworth.

Wechsler, D. (1949), *Wechsler Intelligence Scale for Children*, The Psychological Corporation, New York.

Winnicott, D. W. (1964), *The Child, the Family, and the Outside World*, Penguin, Harmondsworth.

Winnicott, D. W. (1971a), *Therapeutic Consultations in Child Psychiatry*, Hogarth Press, London.

Winnicott, D. W. (1971b), *Playing and Reality*, Tavistock Publications, London.